Dedication

This book is dedicated to my late parents

— Mr and Mrs Dingake

Dintwa.

You toiled to give me education so that I could have a better life.

I owe this to you.

Love you eternally.

IN PURSUIT OF JUSTICE

EXAMINING THE INTERSECTION OF PHILOSOPHY, POLITICS & LAW

Foreword by
HONOURABLE SIR GIBUMA GIBBS SALIKA, KBE CSM
OBE, CHIEF JUSTICE OF PAPUA NEW GUINEA

OAGILE BETHUEL KEY DINGAKE

INDIA · SINGAPORE · MALAYSIA

Notion Press

Old No. 38, New No. 6
McNichols Road, Chetpet
Chennai - 600 031

First Published by Notion Press 2020
Copyright © Oagile Bethuel Key Dingake 2020
All Rights Reserved.

ISBN 978-1-64850-654-3

CONTENTS

FOREWORD

This book by Africa's renowned scholar and judge is bound to get judges and members of the public ferociously debating what are the underlying influences that drive judges to decide matters in a particular way - in particular whether their experience, personal values, education matter at all in the adjudication process. The book also brings to the fore the centuries old debate, on which consensus is rare, being whether judges make law or not! The book serves as a powerful reminder that the work that judges do is complex; and that much as objectivity is a cardinal requirement, in some situations it may be elusive.

Judge Dingake's book comes at a time when the sheer growth of judicial review of executive/legislative actions is seen by some as encroaching into the sphere of the other branches of the state and therefore a violation of the doctrine of separation of powers. In this book, Judge Dingake emphasises the need for judges to respect separation of powers. He also emphasises the importance of judges basing their decisions on law and facts only.

Judge Dingake is both a judge and a scholar. In this book he lets us into his prying and inquisitive thoughts about the intersection of philosophy, politics and law; and his idealised notion of justice comes to the fore. He, like Justice Benjamin Cardazo of the US Supreme Court before him, believes that the ultimate objective of law is the welfare of the people.

This is a stirring and thought provoking book that all those interested in law and the work of judges must read.

I am grateful to Judge Dingake for inviting me to write this foreword to this very thought provoking book. I recommend it strongly to all Judges across the Globe and members of the public.

Sir Gibuma Gibbs Salika, GCL, KBE, CSM, OBE

Chief Justice of Papua New Guinea

Port Moresby, 15th March, 2019

PREFACE

This book is about judges. It discusses the intersection of philosophy politics and law. The vocation of a judge was once described as something akin to priesthood. Even today the idea that judgeship is akin to priesthood subsists because of the belief that judges epitomise righteousness, fairness and justice. Acceptance of the calling is similar to going into monastery – a place of worship occupied by monks living under religious vows.

The values of any civilised society based on the rule of law and democracy depend, to a greater extent, on the faithful performance of judicial duty. These values include liberty, human dignity, peace, order and good governance. Today's judge is required to give effect to the values of a pluralistic society that cherishes democracy, human rights, tolerance and diversity. On occasions, giving effect to the above values may be a function of a judge's experience and background.

In the course of his/her duties, in a country where the Constitution is supreme, the judge must only know and apply one morality – the morality of the Constitution, where every person is equal in the eyes of the law. No one, no constituency, no power block, traditional, religious or otherwise must stand above the Constitution.

A life at the bench is a rare honour and privilege. Some authorities that are religiously inclined have poignantly observed that judgeship is an attribute of God, an assertion not at all surprising given that judges have powers of life and death over their fellow human beings. Those with religious inclination remind us that even God who created the human being, does not sit in judgement over his deeds until their death; and only then does he determine their fate; whether they will be sent to heaven or hell.

The judges' primary responsibility is that which many of us would rather avoid: take decisions. Judges have the grave responsibility to sit in judgment over their fellow human beings in a lifetime. In jurisdictions that still have the death penalty, it is only the judges who can sentence those convicted of heinous crimes to death. It is not uncommon in countries that permit the death sentence that judges' record of imposing the death penalty may differ considerably as to suggest that an individual judge's attitude to the propriety of the death sentence may explain the variance.

In many constitutional democracies it is judges who may have the last word as who is the winner of the disputed elections or whether a president ought to be removed from office. Judges can turn paupers into billionaires and billionaires into paupers. Theirs is a grave responsibility that must be exercised with humility, deep reflection, wisdom and knowledge.

The primary function of a judge is to dispense justice. It has always been a revered principle of liberty and freedom that judges are no respecters of persons but the law; and that they should always stand between the subject and any attempted encroachment on his liberty by the executive, ever vigilant to ensure that any governmental action is justified,

Whilst it is still indisputable that an overwhelming number of cases may be solved largely by a neutral and mechanical application of laws, in some cases of a sensitive political nature, a judge's outlook comes into play to shape the verdict that wins the day. In today's world it is all too common to dress up political problems in legal gab. Judging disputes that may be at an intersection of law and politics can be problematic. Various schools of thoughts such as legal realism, positivism and critical legal studies have attempted to provide tools for understanding the complexity of judging and legal reasoning.

It is a matter of debate whether indeed there are often many answers to a legal problem serving before the courts. Whatever the philosophical answer may be, the reality of the matter is that quite often the judges have a choice between two or more plausible answers.

This book is essentially about how judges tackle difficult questions that lie at the intersection of law and politics. It asserts that judges' ideological outlook may matter in determining the direction of a case in such value laden disputes such as matters of abortion, mercy killing and same sex relationships. The inevitable task of the courts, especially the apex courts, to bridge the gap between law and society, protect the constitution and democracy may be a function of ideological orientation given the truism that no judge ascends to the bench as an ideological virgin.

Chapter One

INTRODUCTION

This book is about judges, philosophy, politics and law and much more. In the pages of this book, which is intended not just for the legal fraternity but for a general readership, I reflect, based on my own experience, and a reading of literature, on how the pursuit of justice lies at the intersection of philosophy, politics and law.

I start off by making a bold assertion: although many judges would deny being political actors, the truth is that they are. Judges political views, as in ideological orientation, not partisan views, color, and often shape their thoughts, and may influence the final decision in a value laden subject like constitutional law. I use the term "ideological" to refer to shared ideas and beliefs. Ideological is an adjective that describes political, cultural, or religious beliefs.

In the United States of America, it is generally accepted that Republican appointed judges tend to be more conservative than those appointed by Democrats in such volatile issues as abortion and same sex relationships. In these value laden cases judges are expected to make sense of often conflicting values, provisions of the law, in order to reach a decision, that is often informed by a judges own ideology, biases and unfortunate and unacceptable as it is – prejudices.

Constitutional law, the field under which issues of abortion and same sex relationships falls, is fundamentally political; and the judges called upon to adjudicate, political actors. To say that judges are political is not to suggest that they are partisan or influenced by partisan politics, which is plainly unacceptable, but to say that broad world outlook of a judge and their broad perspective essentially, on life and social existence matters.

I contextualize my discussion, first, by locating the role of a judge in a democracy, in the context of separation of powers, and then go on to discuss the extent to which the separation of powers constrains the adjudicatory process. I also attempt to answer the question of when judges should defer to the other branches of the state; such as the executive and parliament. Deference is related to separation of powers but does not mean the same thing.

I stretch this discussion further by addressing the question of whether judges make law; and whether the use of international law, by domestic courts, is another way of judges making law, through the back door, or in a manner that is illegitimate. I conclude by discussing the judicialization of politics and the politicization of the judiciary. In augmenting certain observations that I make, in this book, I have drawn on and referred to examples from many different parts of the world; but with a tendency to lean to countries in Sub-Saharan Africa and Kenya; whose jurisdictions I am very familiar with. It is my hope that I reach out to a global general readership and that every citizen of the world who reads this book can relate with some of the perspectives discussed, even if the reader doesn't necessarily agree with what is being said.

It is appropriate, at this early stage, to sketch my judicial path, in broad strokes, to the extent that it advances the broad theme of this book and my background, and again broadly. This is important, because, as it is often said, no judge ascends to the bench as an ideological virgin. I am no exception. I was appointed to the bench at a relatively young age of thirty-nine years. In 2018, after serving a cumulative period of more than fifteen years as judge, of both the Industrial and High Courts of Botswana, I resigned my position to accept an appointment as judge of the Supreme and National Courts of Papua New Guinea; in the Pacific, north of Australia. My decision to leave the service of my home country was motivated not just by a desire to gain appellate court experience; but also to engage with the law in a different social, political and legal milieu.

In the pages of this book, I reflect on my fifteen years' experience as a judge; and attempt to give some theoretical coherence to the job of a judge. I must mention that during my fifteen years as a judge, I have been fortunate enough to combine my judicial functions with academic work; which has always been my passion. I was also fortunate to be recognized and embraced, as an academic, by reputable universities such as the University of Pretoria; where I was privileged to be appointed an 'extra-ordinary law lecturer'. I had the added privilege of being appointed as an honorary Professor of Public Law, by the University of Cape Town, which is a leading university in Africa. In December 2018, I had the honour and privilege to be appointed Adjunct Professor of Law at James Cook University in Australia.

My involvement with academia sharpened my engagement with the law; and has been invaluable to the advancement of my career path. This is because I have kept on learning; and applying the benefits of further education to my work. To the extent that this quest may have, on occasion, brought me into intellectual conflict with the Court of Appeal, in my home country, as some pages of Botswana Law Reports may suggest and other commentary, I have no hesitation in saying that I have tremendously enjoyed seizing the intellectual moment to suggest that there may be other ways of resolving intricate constitutional questions; than those ordinarily employed.

From my judicial experience, I sincerely believe that judgeship can benefit from scholarship that provides new knowledge; and insight into social phenomena and law. This belief emanated from my handling of issues on HIV/AIDS; that often landed on my lap. I came to realize that reading and engaging more with the science of HIV/AIDS, and empirical data, had an impact on the judgements that I delivered. My firm view is that judgements in this area, which are out of step with science and empirical data, are unlikely to serve the ends of justice. If one is to dispense meaningful justice, it helps to be intellectually curious, in matters impacting other disciplines, and seek to know more about those disciplines; to the extent that such pursuit may be relevant. Persistence in the pursuit of knowledge can be rewarding, to the job of a judge, for as long as the judge remembers that judgements are not supposed to be academic pieces; but a practical attempt to legally resolve a concrete dispute serving before the judge.

History teaches that our failure, as people, is our refusal to learn and to reach decisions without much thought as to their rationality and fairness; in all spheres of life. Judges, in particular, cannot afford to take decisions that are not founded on facts and law. They must, at all times, exude knowledge and impartiality. It is this approach that justifies why, judges, although unelected, are granted powers, by most democratic constitutions, to determine issues impacting on the rights and freedoms of the people.

In my experience the broader public is happy to trust the intellect, reason, wisdom and compassion of judges, rather than any other group of people, because of their learning and sense of integrity. It is on this account that I feel confident to assert, without fear of contradiction, that no person should be appointed judge; who has no knowledge of the law and its relationship to justice. Candidates, for the bench, must be tested on their capacity to put the values, and promise, of the constitution into effect. In saying this, I must not be construed to mean that the law, and the judges who apply it, cannot frustrate the aspirations of the people. It would be a mistake to place excessive faith in the law and judges; because they cannot be a panacea for all social ills.

Based on my experience as a judge, of both a national and an international court, and having been sent around Africa, and around the globe, on missions to do with law and justice, I know for certain that, sometimes, it is a grave mistake to repose unlimited confidence in 'wise judges' to resolve what may essentially, and fundamentally, be political questions dressed up as legal questions. By way of example in this regard, I have read judgements, delivered by some of my learned colleagues on the bench, upholding the validity of military takeovers ostensibly because 'the president had unconstitutionally delegated power to unelected officials'. This line of reasoning was supposed to be the justification of why, what was essentially, a coup d'état, was not. I have also read judgments that deny women equal worth to men; and also those that are apologetic about patriarchy and its role in the subjugation of women. I have even read judgements perpetuating the mythology of two genders; namely male and female. Experience has, therefore, taught me that it is not always wise to attribute infallible logic on 'wise judges'.

The point that I am underscoring, by referring to judgements which I have read, concerning infallible logic, is that those appointed to the bench must have the humility to accept that they do not know it all and that, in order to achieve justice, they must subject themselves to continuous learning. This makes it important to have judicial training institutions that are absolutely controlled and run by judiciaries. Another cardinal point that must be emphasized is that judges should appreciate that law is not an end, in itself, but a means to an end; and that, as Benjamin

Cardazo, (1870–1938) of the United States Supreme Court pertinently observed, the ultimate objective of law is the welfare of society. The function of law is to achieve justice and equilibrium. There can be no wisdom in pursuing law at the expense of justice.

Returning to my own experience, in the more than fifteen years that I have served as a judge; I have attempted, as best as I can, to achieve justice according to the law; and not based on my own personal preferences. I have followed a path which I believe to be sacred and correct; namely to sacrifice my own sense of what is wrong or right; for that which the law, and justice, say is wrong or right. This brings to mind a conversation that I once had, with a judicial colleague I hold in the highest respect, which stands in contradiction of the above. I sought to engage him on why colleagues, in his country, were unwilling to protect the public against arbitrary arrests; and what appeared to be land repossessions that were not supported by law. This was after the Southern African Development Community (SADC) Heads of Government decided to shut down the SADC Tribunal in Namibia; an action which, in my mind, amounted to abolishing a court. This followed a politically unpopular decision the Court delivered, that was understood by some people to have undermined the whole purpose of the liberation struggle. My colleague opened up to me and said: "The Judges were afraid; blood was shed for land".

The judge was describing a pre-liberation phase in that country. To his credit, he was very frank in his answer to my question. I derive no pleasure in saying this; but that conversation with my judicial colleague, which has stayed with me, only highlighted the sad fact that a nation which is served by judges who shake in their boots, when the time to effect justice calls, is a lost nation. The same applies to a judiciary that takes political instructions from the executive; or is seen to be too close to the executive. A case in point would be when a Chief Justice is captured giving a bull, as a present, to the head of the executive, as it happened in one Kingdom that produced a Chief Justice who was all too happy to do the bidding of the executive and harass independent minded judges. It does not need to be emphasized that such a gesture, no matter how well intentioned, simply defeats the whole essence of the necessary legal separation between the judiciary and the executive. With this example, it suffices to say that judges who are that close to the executive must be a cause for apprehension.

On my part, I am wedded to the idea that there cannot be any higher honour, for judges, than to defend the independence of the judiciary. In confirmation of this, I find it necessary to mention that, in my life as a servant of the law, I was immensely proud to hear the Chief Justice of Kenya, Honourable David Maraga, say, more than once, that he and his colleagues were prepared to do everything, in their power, to defend the independence of the judiciary. I witnessed this bold, and formidable, stance in defence of the independence of the judiciary when I was privileged to be part of a delegation, of the African Judges and Jurists Forum, (AJJF) that met Honourable Maraga, and his colleagues, following the 2017 Kenyan presidential election petition. It felt extremely good to hear him say that; as that courageous statement roundly epitomized the seriousness that should attach to the defence of independence of the judiciary.

Having briefly outlined some of the necessary attributes that judges must possess in the function of their duties, that is to say integrity, knowledge of the law and impartiality, I now turn to their core accountability, which is that of adjudication. It is no secret that adjudication is a complex assignment; which must be carried out fairly and impartially at all times. The cardinal responsibility that comes with the assignment of adjudication is that, in exercising judicial functions, judges must owe fidelity to the constitution. It is common knowledge that the law is the tool with which adjudicators ply their trade; and that the law is not a science. What may, perhaps, be less obvious is the fact that more often, than not, philosophy and politics impact on how the law is applied to a set of facts; that underpin a particular case. In the following chapters of this book, I look at how the pursuit of justice lies at an intersection of philosophy, politics and law; all of which often collide and collude to produce a particular result, in ways that many people hardly think about.

Chapter Two

THE ROLE OF A JUDGE IN A DEMOCRACY

The plain truth is that whether adjudicating over the fate of a terrorist who bombed an airport or school, or a presidential election petition, or reviewing presidential directives on immigration matters or the immunity of a president, the judge in a modern democracy assumes a role that raises some of the most contentious issues of our time.

A question that is often asked is whether judges are the correct persons to adjudicate over these matters. The answer should be in the affirmative. Judges not being politicians in the ordinary sense of the word, and not owing allegiance to political parties, and not being subject to the authority or influence of anyone, are best placed to adjudicate, because of their assumed independence, learning and impartiality.

An important question that should arise in any discussion on judicial functions is: 'What is the role of a judge in a democracy?' The starting point is, inevitably, that at the heart of formal and substantive democracy are issues concerning sovereignty of the people, the rule of law and human rights. In most countries, particularly in the commonwealth, judges are unelected. The duty to preside over, and determine, disputes is delegated to them, in good faith, by the people; through the mechanism of the constitution. It falls to the courts, in their decisions, not to succumb to the tyranny of the majority; and to have an appreciation of the expansiveness of democracy as an idea; and human construct. It is worth noting that the issue that is often taken is that, somehow, the judiciary is not a democratic institution because the judges are not elected. However, when viewed in the context of the delegated authority that they exercise, this issue is, clearly, without merit. In effect, this is the so called counter-majoritarian argument; which is a favorite line peddled by those who want to delegitimize judicial authority and decisions of the courts.

With the above stated context in mind, it could be said, somewhat simplistically, that the duty of a judge is to decide disputes that serve before him or her, in a manner that does not subvert democracy, the rule of law and human rights. The judge must establish the facts of the case and apply the applicable law. On the face of it, this seems easy enough. But all of us who are familiar with the task of a judge know, from experience, that even the finding of facts can be a complicated and frustrating exercise. Determining which law to apply may be much simpler at times, compared to the process of fact finding.

In the era of constitutional democracy, where political questions dressed up in legal garb, as legal questions, frequent our courts, the task of a judge becomes even more complicated. In some parts of the world, the job of a judge is a perilous one. Taking all this into account, the burning question is: How are judges to determine political questions that have been cast as legal questions? It is important to state that this question is not new. It is perhaps as old as judging itself; the only departure being that, in recent times, it has become more complicated; especially in democracies that are showing signs of fatigue, regression or betrayal of the original promise of what the ideal of democracy entails.

When all the above signs emerge in a democracy, the mistaken temptation to regard the judges as the ultimate messiahs, or saviours, tends to loom large.

As indicated earlier Judges are not, at least in the strict and ordinary sense, politicians. However, whatever the obtaining schools of thought, we cannot run away from the fact that the state, of which judges are top functionaries, is both a political and legal entity. This means that judges must be able to recognize the relationship between law and other disciplines; especially politics, philosophy and sociology. Some scholars have suggested that constitutional law lies at the intersection between politics and law; and they may, indeed, be correct. What can hardly be contested is that the decisions that judges give may have a bearing in advancing, or frustrating, the growth and development of democracy. To this extent, the question that one may pose is: Do judges, in their judgments, advance or constrain the contours of democracy?

In addressing this question, the cardinal issue to be brought to the fore is that the protection of human rights, that is to say the rights of every individual and every minority group, cannot be left in the hands of the legislature and the executive; which by their nature reflect majority opinion. Consequently, the question of the role of the judiciary, in a democracy, arises. The cardinal issue to take note of, in dealing with this question, is that this role must be understood in the context of the reality that the judiciary lacks political, financial and military power. In suggesting, as I do, that judges have a role to play in advancing democracy, I do not wish to be understood, or to mean, to be saying that judges may be partisan. It cannot be over-emphasized that political partisanship is inconsistent with the judicial oath;

as it is the very anti-thesis of impartiality. Judgeship, by its nature, involves fact finding, legal application and legal determination in a dispassionate fashion; which should not be marred by partisanship in any manner or form.

In the majority of cases, legal determination is not problematic. The law is known; and can be easily applied to known facts that are presented before a court. In the words of Montesquieu, the court is but a "mouth that pronounces the words of the law". However, in a few and limited cases, legal determination may not be straight forward. It may involve creation. This simply means that prior to judicial determination, the law may speak in many voices; but after determination, it speaks with one voice; and a new meaning may be created. For instance, in a particular constitution, the phrase *'in accordance with'*, when used prior to the determination of a matter, may mean just that. But after determination, it may mean *'not in accordance with'*.

Similarly, in another constitution, the phrase '*everyone has a right to life*', when used prior to determination of a case, may have meant exactly that, but after determination, it may mean, '*everyone has the right to life – minus the right to water*'. These linguistic intricacies are good examples of when legal determination involves creation.

The notion of ostensible law underscores the role of judges as architects, artists and law makers in certain situations; where such a role becomes imperative. The truth of the matter is that judges are architects who can create 'something' with their own minds. Judges are also artists in that they can create a picture with their own minds and, in the course of interpreting the law, may legislate. In similar vein as has already been observed, that the law is not a science, it is equally true that the law is not mathematics; and judges are not mathematical calculators. Judicial creativity, nay judicial legislation, is natural to law itself; and law, without discretion, is like a body without spirit.

It was Lord Radcliffe who said: "I think that judges will serve the public interest better if they keep quiet about their legislative function". In respectfully differing with this opinion, I don't think judges should keep quiet. To the contrary, they should explain how, or in what way, they make law. The public has a right to know that judges make law; and just how they do it. Justice Holmes, in 1917, said that: "judges do and must legislate". I am in respectful agreement, with this opinion – save to add for clarity that legislate in the sense of legitimate development of the law in the course of interpretation.

A discussion on the legislative functions of judges must, of necessity, interweave with a discussion on the courts and democracy. By their very nature, courts are reflective, and not representative, bodies. They reflect the basic values of a constitution. Engaging with the constitution, inevitably, leads to judges engaging with the concept of democracy; which is an essential element when dealing with issues of the rule of law and good governance. To put this in context, democracy is a complex idea; which is not just about elections or representation. It is also about the human rights of every person. To this end, there is no democracy when the majority takes away the rights of the minority. It needs no emphasis that a cardinal tenet of democracy is that it is about a delicate balance between majority rule and individual rights.

In a constitutional democracy, the constitution delegates, to judges, judicial functions; for the good of society. These functions include the power to interpret statutes and the constitution; and also to develop the common law; which is predominantly judge made. In interpreting statutes and constitutions, the judge is called upon to reflect the values of a constitutional order. These values embody equality, reasonableness, tolerance, justice, proportionality and human rights which, in turn, embody the political, social and economic rights of people. It cannot be over emphasized that, in the exercise of their judicial functions, judges should not be complicit; when society is not faithful to the basic values of the constitution. To exemplify this, when society frowns upon the basic value, or idea, that sexual minorities should not associate; judges should not be complicit. Regardless of their personal views, on the issue, the judges must ensure that justice is served in accordance with the constitution; which they swore to uphold when taking the oath of office. When public opinion is of the view that those alleged to have bombed airports should not be heard; because what they allegedly did was atrocious – the judge should not be complicit. Instead, he or she must honour the values of the constitution; because fair trial and due process also belong to alleged 'terrorists'.

In a nutshell, it is all a matter of judicial balance; and it must be so because human rights are not the only value protected by the constitution. Public order and peace are also basic values; and when these conflict, judges must carry out a delicate balance for the good of society.

Turning the focus to their duties, most of the daily work of judges does not directly impact on the functioning of democracy or any attempt to correct its imperfections. However, on occasion, judges deal with issues that directly impact on the workings of the democratic elections; taking decisions that may be seen as negatively impacting against one section of the population. It is not uncommon to hear of protests; following court decisions on elections or some other issue of national importance. To highlight this point, in June 2018, the Supreme Court of the United States of America (USA), decided, in a narrow majority of 5- 4, to uphold a travel ban imposed on people from some Moslem counties such as Libya, Syria, Iran and Yemen. This judgment resulted in protests in the USA and other parts of the world; as the Supreme Court was deemed to have betrayed the democratic values of the Constitution of the USA. Some scholars hold that this decision was a spectacular betrayal of the constitution; and one not seen in decades. I mentioned, in the preceding chapter, that adjudication is a complex assignment; and it is decisions such as this one, that are an example of some of the hard cases that judges deal with. In the example given, the narrow majority is evidence enough that the decision was not an easy one, for the judges to make, as it involved balancing issues of national security and human rights. Quite often, the right to human dignity, of the individual, conflicts with state security; while that to free speech conflicts with public order or privacy; and it falls on judges to strike the right balance, in their decisions, for the good of society.

Given the above stated scenario, how, then, is it decided which value is of greater importance; and which value supersedes others? Usually, the balancing exercise involves subjective judgement and the exercise of some discretion. It, however, does not follow that a judge is free to do what he, or she, likes. There is no such thing as absolute discretion for judges; for that, surely, would be the beginning of the end of democracy. Each individual judge has a different approach to legal challenges that they are called upon to hear and determine. The balancing act, that judges often undertake, must be a rational process, based on verifiable facts and law.

According to Ronald Dworkin, (1931–2013), the judicial weighing, and balancing, should 'fit' within the normative scheme. Courts cannot afford to be intellectual graveyards of human rights; and neither should they be reckless crusaders of human rights. Recklessness may erode public confidence; which is most undesirable for any functional judiciary. It is, instead, the duty of the courts to provide a steady, balanced and objective intellectual leadership of their communities; devoid of any prejudice or irrationality.

Every generation of judges has its time and moment; a time to be restrained and a time to be proactive. There comes a moment when the courts should lead; and be unflinching in pointing the way forward. There are many examples that come to mind; among them *Brown v Board of Education* in the USA, *LEGABIBO (AG v Rammoge and Others) and Edith Mmusi & 3 Others v. Molefi S. Ramantele & Anor*, in Botswana. The Brown decision abolished racial segregation in schools in the USA, while the LEGABIBO decision in Botswana permitted, for the first time, gay and lesbian people to freely associate and register an association to campaign for their rights. In Mmusi the judge declared that:

"It seems to me that the time has now arisen for the justices of this court to assume the role of judicial midwives and assist in the birth of a new world struggling to be born, a world of equality between men and women as envisioned by the framers of the constitution."

I admit the rhetoric of the above quotation may unsettle some in the bench as it became clear, when the Court of Appeal responded, almost tackling the person of the judge than the ideas the judge painted and the future he envisioned and displayed in words.

Some of the landmark decisions referred to above are, decisions which would probably never have seen the light of day in the judiciaries of yesteryear; but the time and moment were ripe for them to be made.

A judiciary would probably not survive public confidence if it churned out a Brown or LEGABIBO, or Mmusi decision every week; but, by the same token, a judiciary would not survive public confidence if it missed a special moment to have a Brown or LEGABIBO or Mmusi. Needless to say the Brown, LEGABIBO and Mmusi moments must be a function of objectivity; that can withstand scrutiny. Objectivity stands in opposition to the subjective values of a judge. By objectivity, I mean an intellectual process by which a judge reaches beyond himself, or herself, to understand the values that he/she is to weigh and balance. In their judgments, judges should demonstrate that every judgement is a link in a chain; but in so doing, they may be required to build on the residue of the past /tradition; in order to move towards a progressive future in keeping with contemporary norms.

In order to understand the role of a judge in advancing the rule of law in a constitutional democracy, three key issues must be appreciated. The first one is that we must understand what a constitutional democracy is. Secondly, we must have an appreciation of what the rule of law entails and, thirdly, we must define the significance of the rule of law in a constitutional democracy.

Before discussing what is meant by a constitutional democracy, some prior observations that put the issue in context may be appropriate. Following the atrocities occasioned by the Second World War, a period that was characterized by massive violations of human rights, a wave of new thinking of what a democracy entailed started to emerge. The new conceptualization of democracy understood that the concept of democracy could not begin, and end, with elections that were organized on a regular basis of say four or five years. It was understood that democracy should be participatory, responsive, and accountable and, above all else, must respect human rights.

A fundamental lesson arising out of the ravages of the Second World War was that the people, through their representatives, could destroy democracy and human rights. We now know, as a result of the ravages of the Second World War, that without human rights, we cannot talk of democracy. The protection of human rights, especially the rights of minorities and other marginalized groups, cannot be left to the legislatures and executives alone. History is replete with examples of how these two branches of government have more often, than not, disappointed when it came to promoting, protecting, fulfilling and upholding rights.

In discharging their functions judges should not be partisan; or politically inclined; but neither should they be apolitical. Some judges may be unsettled by the idea that judges should not be apolitical. This may be on account of many factors relating to their understanding of what politics entails; and what being apolitical, in particular, means. In the same vein, different judges would answer the question on the role of a judge in a democracy differently. This is perfectly normal. Ideological pluralism, and not uniformity, is the hall mark of the judiciary in a democratic society. It is always better, if justice is to be achieved, to have a hundred schools of thought blossom, springing from these divergent ideological outlooks.

Judges function better in societies that are democratic. Societies that are not democratic cannot harness the best in a judiciary that is trained to ensure that the rights of every person are upheld. Aside this, a democracy that does not guarantee the independence of the judiciary, for instance, cannot promote, protect, fulfill or uphold the human rights of every person. Put somewhat bluntly, and perhaps inelegantly, a deficient democracy is bad for the rule of law. A democracy in which conditions do not exist for judges to be independent cannot produce the best democratic yield. A democracy in which judges become the gate keepers of the executive, or judges become willing, and subservient, tools to advance party political agendas, is a deformed one.

Returning to its definition, a constitutional democracy is a system where the government is both constitutional and democratic in nature. It is, therefore, a combination of two concepts (constitutionalism and democracy) which make up a constitutional democracy. In order to provide a clear definition of a constitutional democracy, it is important to briefly define the idea of a constitutional government and a democratic government. A 'constitutional government' relates to government according to the terms of the constitution. However, the fact that there is a formal constitution, according to whose provisions government business is conducted, does not, in itself, mean that such a government is a constitutional one. This is because for a government to qualify as a constitutional one, its constitution must have the force of a supreme, overriding law; imposing limitations upon the power of the government and in practice, the government must adhere to those limitations.

Since the 19th century, various definitions of the term 'democracy ' have been suggested. The underlying idea of a democratic government is the popular basis upon which the government is founded and operates. In other words, the government must be based upon the free consent of the governed, given by means of a free, fair and credible election conducted at regular periodic intervals. In addition, a democratic government subscribes to the rule of law. The veteran jurist, Albert Venn Dicey, defined the rule of law as the principle that the actions of government must be based upon the law; and the law must treat all persons equally. Since the years of Dicey, the principle of the rule of law has developed two sides to it, namely the formal and the substantive aspects. The formalist side of the rule of law, also known as the principle of legality, requires a government to act in accordance with the law.

The substantive side of the rule of law is concerned with the nature, or content, of the law. Earlier on, it was pointed out that a constitutional democracy is a government based upon constitutional values such as respect for fundamental human rights and freedoms. Flowing from this, in a constitutional democracy, the substantive side of the rule of law requires the law to capture and embody such democratic values as respect for fundamental human rights and separation of powers, and requires all exercise of public power to respect and promote those values. Thus, in a constitutional democracy, the rule of law is, essentially, a principle which obliges governments to act in accordance with the law; and which requires the law to capture and advance the essential tenets and values of constitutional

democracy. In casting this in a clearer light, it is of importance to note that the observance of the principle of the rule of law must be understood as a constitutive element of a constitutional democracy.

The rule of law is, however, not just a constitutive element of constitutional democracy. It is also the vehicle through which the constitutional limitations imposed upon a government are applied. It is the ultimate mechanism limiting the whims of rulers; by subordinating their acts to the law. For instance, where a constitution requires that the exercise of government power to be done in accordance with respect for fundamental human rights and freedoms, it is through the application and enforcement of the rule of law that such constitutional limitations will take effect; and serve their purpose of preserving human liberty. Furthermore, in its general application, the rule of law ensures that citizens and government are subjected to the supremacy of the law. It also ensures that the conduct of government, and its citizens, is within the confines of the law; and the limitations imposed by the constitution itself.

Without the rule of law, government officials, and other powerful citizens would act as they pleased; which, in turn, would attract disastrous consequences on democracy and individual rights and freedoms. The application and enforcement of the rule of law is, therefore, as important to the survival of constitutional democracy; as the supply of oxygen is critical to the survival of the human body. Without the rule of law, governments would cease to adhere to constitutional limitations, with the result that there would be no constitutional democracy to talk about.

Reflecting further, the role of judges, in a constitutional democracy, is to enforce the rule of law; particularly the constitution. One may ask how this is achieved. The answer is that judges enforce the rule of law when they adjudicate over disputes that are brought before their courts. Earlier on, I likened the significance of the rule of law, in a constitutional democracy, to how the supply of oxygen is important to the survival of the human body. However, I hasten to point out, and I daresay that scientists reading this would most probably like nothing better than to tan my hide for this, that enforcing the rule of law is a complex task, which is far from being as simple and automatic as the normal act of inhaling oxygen and exhaling carbon dioxide; by a human body. I say this because enforcing the rule of law is a responsibility that involves the complex task of interpreting legal provisions, balancing competing constitutional values and withstanding political pressure; all of which require a judiciary that is independent, impartial, courageous and prudent.

In order to advance the rule of law, judges have three key roles namely; interpreting the law appropriately, actively developing the law to give effect to the values underlying the constitutional democratic system and asserting their independence as a branch of the constitutional government. It will be in order to explain each of these roles separately. One of the challenges to the rule of law, in contemporary constitutional democracies is the attempt by governments, and other political players, to control the judiciary. Despite the fact that constitutions, generally and unambiguously, guarantee the independence of the judiciary, politicians and powerful business persons continue to make maneuvers that are intended to capture the judiciary; and to ensure that the judges give judgments that are favorable to governments and other powerful individuals. It is, therefore, an understatement to say that the independence and impartiality of the judiciary is essential for the enforcement and advancement of the rule of law.

Judges ought to remember, at all times, that they have a duty to assert their own independence; and the best way to achieve this is to ensure that they always give impartial judgments. What is meant by this? It is simply that impartial judgments are not necessarily decisions which are against the government; or which are sympathetic to public opinion. Impartial decisions are verdicts that are based on the law and nothing else. Whilst the view, which holds that the success of constitutionalism depends on the judicious politics of the court to establish its democratic legitimacy, through cooperation and collaboration with the other branches of government, cannot be faulted, so should the belief, be upheld, that the judiciary must not, under any circumstances, abdicate from its constitutional duty to enforce the law. The judiciary must refuse to countenance behavior that threatens the rule of law and constitutional democracy. Notwithstanding any pressure from within, or outside, government, judges must always remember that they are the guardians of the prescriptions of the constitution and, as such, they have the fundamental responsibility to stand firm and defend the constitution.

Although it almost always occupies a top slot in that regard, political interference is not the only challenge that confronts the judges in executing their role of enforcing the rule of law. Interpretation of the law itself presents fundamental challenges. As such, judges are often confronted with a challenge regarding the true and correct meaning of the legal provisions in a given context. It is a truism that when interpreting legislation, the judges must

deduce the meaning of the law from the language or grammar used. The difficulty of this, however, is that the text of the law does not always have a single and fixed meaning. Interpreting legal provisions, like the legislation, often involves two stages. The first stage is when judges have to find all the possible meanings; which have a textual anchor in the norm that is subject to interpretation. The second stage is when the judge exercises the discretion to prefer and adopt a meaning which materializes the purpose of the text.

When choosing the relevant meaning of legal provisions, judges ought to member that their role is to promote and protect the values underlying the constitutional democratic system. Consequently, they must prefer the meaning which gives full effect to such constitutional values. Another facet of the interpretation of legal provisions, which poses another challenge to judges, is in relation to new constitutions. In circumstances where a new constitution is promulgated, most of the legislation is out of step with the provisions of the new constitution; and it takes time for the legislature to realign such legislation with the new constitution. Faced with these circumstances, judges have a responsibility to exercise a degree of activism to interpret, or develop, the law so that it gives full effect to the values underlying the constitutional democratic system.

It should be noted that even in mature constitutional democracies, where the legislature has already realigned the legislation with the constitution, the judges are still confronted with legislation that has gaps in it. Judges, thus, have the responsibility to fill such gaps; in consideration of the legislative purpose, and when discharging such a responsibility, the judges exercise discretion in choosing the appropriate way of filling in those gaps. More often than not, there is a way of filling those gaps which favours the status quo. But, conversely, there is also another way which displeases the status quo. In spite of this, judges must recall that they are the custodians of the constitution; and they must, with courage and firmness, fill in those gaps in a manner that gives full effect to the aspirations and values of the constitution.

One outstanding trait of democracy is that, by its nature, it does not guarantee that the best skilled persons will become the legislators; or leaders in the executive. Many times, we have witnessed people being elected into Parliament, who are without any knowledge of, or skill around, lawmaking. Such technical shortcomings, of the legislators, contribute towards the enactment of high volumes of legislation; which do not adequately give effect to the spirit, object and purpose of the constitution, and which also do not sufficiently capture the values underlying the constitutional democratic system. This is in direct conflict with the rule of law; which requires that legislation must adequately give effect to those underlying constitutional values. As such, it is the duty of the judges to develop an interpretation, of such legislation, which gives clear effect to those constitutional values. In instances where legislation exists, which is not capable of an interpretation, that duly gives effect to those values, then the judges must be bold enough to strike down the relevant provisions of that legislation; or read in certain provisions that will enable the legislation to give effect to the constitutional values. In the absence of such judicial activism, the rule of law will circumvented; and the legislation will not serve its intended purpose; for the good of the people.

In many jurisdictions in Southern Africa, the common law remains a source of law; and relevant principles of this law must be applied to resolve legal disputes. Notwithstanding the existence of judicial precedents, common law, largely, remains a loose body of unwritten, age old, legal principles. There is no 'one size fits all' body of common law; that is ready to be utilized to resolve every legal dispute that comes before the courts. When judges apply common law to resolve a dispute, they have to search and determine the relevant norms; and then interpret such norms appropriately. For, instance, in terms of the constitution of Zimbabwe, judges have a duty to interpret, and develop, common law; in manner that promotes the spirit and objectives of the Bill of Rights. The spirit and objective of the Bill of Rights is to ensure that individuals fully enjoy the fundamental rights enshrined therein. As such, the judges ought to develop common law principles in a manner that promotes such constitutional values like respect for human rights and the rule of law.

In 2013, in Zimbabwe, an interesting case served before the Constitutional Court; with grave implications for democracy and the rule of law. The applicant, in that case, requested the court to make an order that elections be held on a date prior to 25th July 2013. The case implicated two constitutional values; and the judges had to prefer one over the other. One value was that in a constitutional democracy, elections must be held within the constitutionally defined time frame. On the other hand, the same constitutional democracy required that elections must be free and fair; and that certain preparations must be done before the elections were conducted. In terms of the Constitution of Zimbabwe, such preparations would include conducting an intense voter registration process; prior to the holding of the elections.

This case is a typical example of the complexity of the task of constitutional adjudication, where judges have to weigh and balance competing constitutional values. In such scenarios, different political actors will be expecting the court to prefer one value over the other. However, it is not the duty of the judges to please any of those actors.

As was pointed out earlier on, a common feature of most constitutions is that they require the judiciary to exercise fidelity to the law. Most constitutions in Southern Africa, especially those that were crafted in the last twenty years, or so, provide that the courts are independent and are subject to the constitution and the law; which they must apply impartially. This entails that judges have no obligation to prefer a constitutional interpretation that favours any of the political players; regardless of whether such politicians are in government or in opposition. Rather, the judges must look deeper into the competing constitutional values; and give priority to the constitutional value that is more significant and relevant for the survival and flourishing of an open and democratic constitutional state.

Most contemporary constitutional democracies require the judiciary to consider international and foreign law when interpreting the provisions of the constitution; particularly those that have to do with the protection and promotion of fundamental human rights. The former Chief Justice of South Africa once held that international law provides a framework and guidance within which the Bill of Rights can be evaluated and understood. I cannot agree more with that assertion.

International law consists of a rich body of legal principles, relating to human rights, which domestic courts can refer to; in order to interpret and develop the content of human rights provisions in the constitution, common law and statutes. When adjudicating, judges ought to refer extensively to international law; in order for their interpretation, of the constitution, to benefit from this rich human rights jurisprudence. Of course, the provisions within international law agreements must be interpreted within the historical context of a particular country; and not in a vacuum. Nonetheless, judges must learn as much as they can from international law human rights jurisprudence; in order to promote the rule of law in their respective countries.

In conclusion, let me say that the application of the law, to resolve disputes, is the essence of the idea of the rule of law. If the law is not applied, then there is no way that the law can rule. Judges are, thus, mandated to apply the law and ensure that it rules. However, they ought not to lose sight of the fact that applying the law requires diligent interpretation and development of the law. The central role of judges in advancing the rule of law is to interpret and develop the law; in a manner that secures, protects and promote the values underlying the constitutional democratic system.

It is clear from this narrative that the state of a country's democracy is what shapes and informs the role of a judge, to ensure that the rule of law prevails at all times; and that individual rights are respected. A judge must avoid giving effect to unjust laws; if it is possible to do so by legitimately construing the constitution in accordance with the principles of international law. A judge must avoid being a lapdog of the executive; and must similarly shun giving expression to undemocratic values; especially where there are many competing ones, among which are values that are restrictive of human rights. Constitutions are meant to be dynamic; and to serve the aspirations of the current generations and of those yet unborn. Consequently, the meanings that are attached to constitutional text are bound to change with time. By way of example, an interpretation, given to a particular text, which has remained unchanged, for the last hundred years, may give way to a new meaning a hundred years later. In essence, the meaning of a provision, of the law, is influenced by time and environment. It is relative and incomplete.

Honing in on the question that was posed, earlier, on the role of judges in a democracy, the response always ought to be that judges must play a role in bridging the gap between law and society. In many ways a judge, although not a primary law-giver, is an important partner in law making. He or she, irons out the creases; and as Lord Denning, (1899–1999), once said, "which ironing may yield a refined legal norm; and he fills gaps in the law and often lays a new precedent – a new law. As a law maker, his law making, must be informed; and he should not legislate, willy-nilly. He must legislate within bounds, and in accordance with accepted legal precepts. In his lawmaking he has a duty to maintain the coherence of the legal system as a whole".

At the end of it all the role of a judge in a democracy involves objectivity and balancing many competing values.

The judge in doing the balancing exercise is not accountable to public opinion or politicians, but the fundamental values of the rule of law. Judges and scholars steeped in the rule of law and constitutionalism would agree that the role of a judge in a democracy often causes tensions amongst the three arms of the state; but that those tensions are natural and often healthy. Ultimately, the judge's role in a democracy is to protect the constitution in a way that serves democratic values

Chapter Three

SEPARATION OF POWERS

The judiciary is an organ of state and judges state functionaries who must operate within the boundaries prescribed by the constitution. It is an important constitutional imperative that the judiciary, which is one of three basic and equal pillars in the modern democratic state, should function independently of the other two: the legislature and executive. The relationship between the three branches of government should be characterized by mutual respect, each recognizing and respecting the proper role of the others. This is absolutely imperative because the judiciary has an important role and functions in relation to the other two branches. It ensures that the executive, the legislature and other entities are held to account for their actions.

It is the judiciary that is constitutionally mandated to ensure that the legislature does not pass any laws it wishes to enact, but only those permitted and authorized by the constitution. To fulfil its role in these respects, and to ensure a completely free and unfettered exercise of its independent legal judgment, the judiciary must be truly independent and impartial and not subject to any control of any authority whether public or private.

History has taught humanity that unlimited power in the hands of one authority is dangerous and inimical to national interest. The idea of separation of powers in a democracy is meant to prevent abuse of power and to safeguard freedom for all people. The system of separation of powers allocates powers to the three branches of government: executive, legislative and judiciary. These three branches must exercise checks and balances on each other.

The idea of separation of powers has a long history. Most of this history reflects problems concerning the nature of government in England in the seventieth century. Scholars and commentators of various shades have written and spoken about separation of powers for centuries. Academic disagreements have often arisen as to whether it was John Locke, (1632–1704), the Englishman or the French philosopher Montesquieu, (1689–1755), who came up with the concept of separation of powers. For our purposes and without taking sides, it is sufficient to remind ourselves of the elementary wisdom posited by Montesquieu, in his acclaimed treatise *L'Espirit de Lois,* where he discussed the doctrine of separation of powers. His central argument was that the separation of powers amongst the executive, the legislature and the judiciary was the condition precedent for liberty. According to Montesquieu, if one authority exercised executive, legislative, and judicial powers, then that would be the very definition of tyranny.

Separation of powers requires the three arms of the state to keep to their designated mandate and not to trespass into another's function. The legislature has no mandate to make a law that infringes the constitution; the executive has no power to formulate and implement policy that is contrary to law and the judiciary has no power to formulate policy for the governance of the country. The Legislature must only make laws permitted by the constitution; and both the legislature and the executive must defer to the judgment of the court in any conflict generated by an enactment challenged on constitutional grounds.

If the legislature makes laws that offend against the constitution and refuses to defer to the judgment of the court, it is in breach of its mandate. A democratic legislature has no option to ignore or subvert the court order; it must either accept its judgment, or seek an appropriate amendment of the law, without subverting the basic foundations of the constitution.

It is generally accepted that policy conception, design and implementation is the province of the executive. Quite often different legal tools can be used to implement policy. Policy may be contained in legislation or it may take the form of executive and/or presidential directives addressed to government bureaucrats to implement. These different tools have different constitutional and legal implications. As a general rule, the law requires that although policy conception, formulation and design is a function of the executive it must comply with constitutional constraints such as legality, rationality and the Bill of Rights.

It is a requirement of the law that all government conduct must have a legal foundation. This is often called the principle of legality which asserts that the legislature and executive in every sphere are constrained by the principle that they may exercise no power and perform no function beyond that conferred by law. The principle of the legality is an important component of the rule of law. The rule of law requires that the exercise of public power must be exercised in accordance with the constitution and the law. It follows that where policy is not authorized by law it cannot pass constitutional scrutiny.

The second constraint is the rationality test. The rationality test requires that there be some nexus or link between the purpose sought to be achieved by relevant action and the legislation in question. Where there is no link or the link is illegitimate then the relevant action complained of would be irrational. It follows from the above that a decision that is objectively irrational cannot be sanctioned by the courts. The requirement of rationality does not permit the courts to substitute their opinions as to what would be appropriate for that of the government.

The third constraint is that of the bill of rights. All government policy, whether contained in legislation or presidential directives, may not infringe the rights entrenched in the bill of rights. The legislature, the executive, as well as the judiciary, are all bearers of obligations under the Bill of Rights; which means that they are duty bound to protect and fulfill them. It is not the role of the courts to frustrate, and sabotage, the executive in carrying out its constitutional mandate to rule. The place of the courts is to hold it accountable for the manner in which the executive exercises public power. In doing this, the courts need to approach judicial review with heightened sensitivity to the imperative of separation of powers. They must understand, and recognize, that their primary duty is to ensure that government works in terms of the constitution and the law. Other than ensuring compliance with the constitution and the law, everything else is not the business of the courts. The reasons for this are obvious. Firstly, the legislature and indirectly, the executive, are democratically elected and the courts are not. Secondly, courts are institutionally ill-equipped to make complex policy decisions.

Judicial interventions predicated on pure judicial adventurism, and not consistent with legal discipline, logic and common sense can be counter-productive and yield chaotic consequences. It is the principle of constitutional supremacy that will dictate the interaction of the judiciary and the executive; when dealing with the question of separation of powers. Quite often, the judiciary is criticized as 'counter-majoritarian', as it is not elected. This criticism should not intimidate the courts. It is the constitutional mandate of the courts to uphold the constitution. There is no doubt that the phenomenal growth of the courts' power to review executive and legislative action, and set them aside where appropriate, can, if used unprofessionally, be destructive. But if properly used, this power of review can help in building and maintaining a society based on the rule of law. In a functioning constitutional democracy, the courts must resist being reduced into mere paper tigers; with the capacity to snarl and roar; but no teeth with which to bite and no sinews to execute their judgments.

Many judges and lawyers would readily agree that whilst the idea of separation of powers is generally accepted, experience has shown that the actual application of the doctrine differs from country to country. Different courts have developed their own unique model of separation of powers; i.e. one that is consistent with their history and circumstances. Notwithstanding the varying models of separation of powers, the essence generally remains the same, namely, the need to distribute power to different arms of the state, and to ensure that these different arms of the state exercise checks and balances on each other. It is a critical aspect of this doctrine that, at the end of the day, separation of powers should not be such as to make it difficult for government to govern.

Some constitutions, especially those crafted in the 1950 and 60's, do not even mention the doctrine of separation of powers. However, when reading these constitutions, one realizes that there are separate provisions relating to the executive, the legislature and the judiciary. An example that comes to mind is Botswana. In that country, the constitution does not have any express provision on the separation of powers; but the courts have held that, reading the constitution as a whole, it is clear that there is separation of powers in Botswana. Aside the decisions of the courts, the fact that separation of powers, in Botswana, is not explicitly provided for, in the constitution, does not diminish its effect and force. The court's finding that there was separation of powers, notwithstanding it not being expressly provided for, was based on a consideration of the structure and provisions of the constitution. In law, an implicit provision of the constitution does not have any less force than an express provision. In determining that separation of powers existed, in Botswana, the Court of Appeal held that, having regard to structure and provisions of the constitution, which dealt with the three organs of the state, the separation of powers was a loose one. This was manifested by the fact that members of the executive were drawn from the legislature; and there was, as such, the occasional overlapping of powers.

Carrying the issue further, most constitutions do not aspire for an absolute separation of powers. They contemplate, instead, that there would, inevitably, be an overlapping of powers, amongst the three arms of the government; which often results in confusion. To insist on bright lines, in the constitution, demarcating the province of each is extremely difficult, if not impossible. This difficulty explains why there are checks and balances, in place, to ensure that each organ of the state tries to keep to its own lane; as much as practicably possible. One of the main reasons why most constitutions do not aspire for an absolute separation of powers is because interaction amongst the branches of government is unavoidable. It is, in fact, necessary; if kept to within reasonable limits. This interaction becomes evident, for instance, when the courts strike out a piece of legislation as being unconstitutional; and parliament responds by amending the offending legislation in order for it to comply with the constitution. This is the ideal situation; which should be a standard practice in a well-functioning democracy. However, the reality is very different in that what is often done by legislatures, after a court strikes a piece of legislation as being unlawful, is to seek to pass legislation which overrules the court; rather than to remedy the defects, identified by the court, that led to the piece of legislation being strike out.

In order for a system of checks and balances, as envisioned by the constitution, to work effectively, and with minimal friction, it is important that the three organs of the state understand the founding values of the constitution and that, where there is a controversy about what each branch can or cannot do, the courts are the ones that must finally pronounce on the boundaries of each. The other branches must understand that the role of giving life to the foundational values is a clear function of the courts; and should not be subject to any debate.

It is a necessary component of the doctrine of separation of powers that courts have a constitutional duty to ensure that the exercise of power, by other branches of government, occurs within constitutional limits. Flowing from this, it needs to be emphasized that when it comes to respecting and ensuring compliance with the constitution, all the three arms of the state have an equal obligation to ensure compliance. The fact that the courts are the final authority, with regard to interpreting the constitution, does not mean that the other branches have no duty to respect the constitution.

It is absolutely imperative that all the arms of the state must individually, and collectively, work towards giving effect to the provisions of the constitution. Essentially, they must all have one mission; which is to uphold the constitution. It is unfortunate that a perception is often created, for instance, that concern about human rights should be the sole pre-occupation of the judiciary; and not the other branches. To the contrary, if the constitution is to be more meaningful to the lives of people, then the three arms of the state must, continuously, be in conversation with each other. This is what, in literature, is called constitutional dialogue.

The idea that all the branches of government must have one mission, that being to uphold the constitution, has not always been there. Traditionally, the thinking was that these three branches had their respective areas of operation to guard; and nothing in common. However, the reality that is emerging, these days, is that the three branches of the government are always defining, and re-defining, their shared borders. They are, increasingly, realizing they all have an obligation to uphold the constitution. As indicated earlier, the separation of powers, in the constitution, is not carved in bright colours; but over time, it has been made much clearer by continual engagement and interaction between the three organs of the state.

A number of constitutions, in most democracies, grant courts the power to declare legislation, which is inconsistent with the constitution, to be invalid to the extent of the inconsistency. An order of nullification, of such legislation, is a form of communication between the judiciary and the legislature; to which the latter quite often responds. Where appropriate, the legislature may extend the conversation to the principals, that is to say the voters, before it responds to a nullification order. A good example of the conversation between the courts and the legislature happened in South Africa in, or about, 2006 in the case of Lesbian and Gay Equality Project v Minister of Home Affairs; where the court held that certain provisions of the Marriage Act, in that country, were inconsistent with the constitution; to the extent that they failed to make provisions for ensuring that same sex couples enjoyed the same status as heterosexual couples. After handing down its verdict, the court gave the South African parliament twelve months in which to address the defect in the Marriage Act; which the court had identified.

Another interesting example is that provided by the South African case of Zondi v MEC for Traditional and Local Government Affairs. The issue that arose, in the case, concerned the constitutional validity of the Provincial Ordinance which, among other things, provided for the seizure and impoundment of trespassing animals. The court held that certain provisions of the Ordinance were inconsistent with the constitution. In considering the appropriate remedy, the court found that it was not well placed to cure the inconsistency; and that the appropriate body to do that was the legislature. As it had done in the Lesbian and Gay Equality case, the court similarly gave the provincial legislature of Kwazulu Natal twelve months to respond to the issue of the Ordinance's inconsistency with the constitution. Some eleven months after the judgment, the provincial legislature approached the court for an extension of time in which to respond. This is a very healthy example of a functioning constitutional dialogue in a democracy.

It must be emphasized that even as the separation of powers is discussed, the keeping of state organs to their individual designated lanes is cardinal. In that regard, it is clearly not the mandate of the courts to frustrate government; in its policies to improve the welfare of the people. In terms of the principles of constitutional law, the court has no right to formulate government policy, but it does have the right to adjudicate on the question of whether or not the implementation of a government policy results in the deprivation of human rights. In the era of a welfare state, the functions of government are numerous and pervasive; and it can very safely be said that everywhere that one turns to, there is likely to be government presence and influence. This is because governments, all over the world, are increasingly becoming involved in issues of social welfare; such as providing food rations, school fees, houses, pensions, employment and health facilities. As a result of the growth in the functions of the modern state, the judiciary often finds itself deciding cases with social policy implications.

When deciding such cases, as have been referred to above, which have social policy implications, the courts may be faced with a myriad of challenging and complex questions. For instance, does the right to life and liberty mean that a brain dead individual has the right to remain on life support for decades? Should state workers be entitled to a cost of living adjustment every year? Do workers in the private sector have a legitimate expectation to share in the profits of the employer; where it is shown that their productivity contributed immensely to the profits reached? In such circumstances, the elephant in the room to be addressed is: are these matters not best resolved through democratic debates, negotiation and compromise? Is it proper for judges to be involved in matters of social policy? Do they have the capacity to do so? When the judges find themselves entangled in matters of policy, does that not amount to trespassing into the province of the legislature?

These questions are real. I am sure that I speak for many judges when I state that, quite often, a judge may find himself/herself wondering whether their intervening in a particular dispute is not tantamount to undermining another branch of the State. In answer to this, I would say that when such a question arises, judges often try their best to seek the right balance. They may not often get this right, despite their best efforts, and when that happens, it is legitimate for the elected representatives to let the judiciary know of their failure to strike a balance on the issue on which their intervention was sought, in a debate in Parliament. What all this shows is that, invariably, the functions of the various arms of government do overlap, and that those in the three organs of the state need to cooperate, and to be cautious of the boundaries of their responsibilities, in order to ensure that the three branches do not undermine each other. They owe it to the public to do so. It is very important that the public has confidence in the three organs of the state; and that they, in turn, remain faithful to their constitutional mandate. For the judiciary, public confidence is its life blood.

As is often said, the value of the judiciary lies in its members' intellectual insight, impartiality and integrity.

In Africa, various models on the separation of powers have been adopted; as demonstrated, hereunder, by reference to the models adopted in Botswana, South Africa, Kenya and Uganda. The majority of post-independence constitutions embody various models of separation of powers. However, over time, these provisions have been systematically weakened, revised, suspended and/or replaced with ones that concentrate power in the executive branch. It is a sad reality that one of the major challenges confronting good governance, in Africa, is how to effectively constrain the executive's power and creatively balance its discretionary authority; without diluting its ability to fulfil its constitutional obligations and political mandate, and to perform its functions efficiently and effectively.

As has already been mentioned, in most, if not all constitutional democracies in Africa, judges are not elected democratically; and they do not have to account to an electorate. Consequently, the judiciary enjoys some measure of protection, from political process, when accomplishing its constitutional mandate. The notion of judicial independence, thus, aims to forestall overt government influence on the judiciary. It also aims to ensure that the judiciary makes decisions in accordance with the rule of law; and the requirements of justice.

Botswana is usually lauded as Africa's oldest continuous democracy, as a result of having enjoyed decades of a peaceful multi - party system; since gaining her independence in 1966. It may be correct to observe that this success is tempered by growing concerns that the country's remarkable stability has come at the cost of further political development. Significant weaknesses in Botswana's democracy include low civic participation, relatively weak opposition and civil society sectors, and a lack of incumbent turnover in consecutive free and fair elections.

One of the most crucial features of any modern constitutional democracy is judicial control over the executive. I hasten to add that the term 'control', as used in this context, is not to mean, or even remotely suggest, that the judiciary is superior to the other organs of government. It is used to demonstrate a working separation of powers; through one organ of the state providing the necessary checks and balances to ensure that another state organ performs its statutory duties in keeping with its mandate and boundaries; for the good of the people. In Botswana, judicial control over executive action is exercised regularly, and quite successfully I might add, in order to protect its citizens from any unlawful acts of government officials, or departments, by ensuring that they perform their statutory duties without exceeding their powers. On several occasions, the Botswana courts have nullified governmental acts that they considered to be unlawful.

Although the doctrine of separation of powers, alone, cannot explain Botswana's exemplary record as a successful, liberal, multi-party, constitutional democracy, in Africa, its impact cannot be ignored. The executive, especially the Office of the President, is as powerful as any in Africa; but what sets Botswana apart from most other African governments, is the considerable freedom with which the courts regularly review and invalidate irregular and illegal executive and legislative acts. Individuals who feel that their constitutional rights have been infringed have regularly resorted to the courts.

Africa's other promising democracy is South Africa. That country enacted an admirable and sophisticated liberal democratic constitution after the end of apartheid. The provisions include full voting rights for all, a judicially enforceable bill of rights, fundamental individual freedoms and independent, democracy enhancing, institutions and watchdogs. More significantly, the constitution of South Africa provides, specifically, for judicial authority to be vested in the courts. It provides that:

1. The judicial authority of the Republic is vested in the courts.

2. The courts are independent and subject only to the constitution and the law; which they must apply impartially and without fear, favour or prejudice.

3. No person, or organ of state, may interfere with the functioning of the courts.

4. Organs of state, through legislative and other measures, must assist and protect the courts to ensure the independence, impartiality, dignity, accessibility and effectiveness of the courts.

5. An order or decision issued by a court binds all persons to whom and organs of state to which it applies.

The constitution of South Africa also provides for a series of checks and balances against presidential and executive overreach; including term limits and separation of powers. In spite of the progressiveness of its constitution, the success story of South Africa has not been without tribulations. The judiciary, which is, arguably, the most crucial barrier that the constitution erected to prevent political overreach, has been subject to huge pressures for transformation. Furthermore, and although the judiciary has delivered many key, and controversial, decisions that hold the executive to account, judges have been increasingly subjected to attacks whenever their judgments have gone against the interests of the ruling African National Congress (ANC) party and its leaders.

Kenya and Uganda, on the other hand, have often been characterized, in literature, as quasi-democracies; which have held consecutive elections in the post-independence years, but still face significant challenges in meeting the ideals of liberal democracy; particularly the rule of law, the separation of powers and, most crucially, independent judiciaries. These two countries have gone through several constitution building processes, and there is hope that some of the newer provisions will serve to insulate the judiciary from executive interference. Scholars have noted that Kenya has been afflicted by the 'big man' syndrome, and not institutions; which is a situation that has forged Kenya's uneven path to democracy. As such, Kenya's strong central authority, a holdover from the colonial period, keeps the judiciary, parliament, and the electoral commission subservient to the president.

A noteworthy development is that under its new constitution, the Kenyan judiciary is, primarily, charged with the responsibility of ensuring that there is fair and effective administration of justice. It also provides a safeguard against the abuse of power; by the other arms of the state. In the performance of their mandate, judges and other judicial officers are guided by specific principles; which include the non-discriminatory delivery of justice; expeditious delivery of justice; promotion of alternative forms of dispute resolution; de-emphasis of procedural technicalities; as well as protection and promotion of the purpose and principles of the 2010 constitution.

In Uganda, the courts have valiantly produced jurisprudence that seeks to flesh out and inculcate the values espoused in the constitution. However, the courts do not operate in a vacuum. In the past, a number of fact finding missions to Uganda, including one by the International Bar Association (IBA) have noted many areas that threatened judicial independence; including government officials' repeated criticism of judicial decisions; and defiance to comply with them. Another area noted, that threatened judicial independence in Uganda, concerned allegations that some members of the judiciary are pressured into colluding with the state police; for the arrest of opposition politicians. Also noted was the issue of cases of government officials' direct interference with the discharge of the duties of the judiciary. The IBA delegation observed that understaffing, and chronic underfunding of the judiciary, presented severe obstacles to the functioning and independence of the institution.

Like many other countries, Uganda aspires for judicial independence. In concretizing that aspiration, the constitution of Uganda guarantees judicial independence in article 128. With regard to the organizational structure of the judiciary, the Chief Justice, the Deputy Chief Justice, the Principal Judge and judges of the Supreme Court, the Court of Appeal and the High Court are all appointed by the President; acting on the advice of the Judicial Service Commission; and with the approval of Parliament.

As for their tenure of service, the judges remain in office until they are seventy (70) years old; and may retire on reaching the age of sixty (60). Turning to the question of removal from office, article 144 of the Ugandan constitution stipulates that a judge may be removed, by the President, only on the grounds of inability to perform the functions of his or her office, arising from infirmity of body or mind; misbehaviour, misconduct or incompetence. At a formal level, the constitution of Uganda vests judicial power in the judiciary; in clearer terms than most other constitutions do. Article 126(1) of the Ugandan constitution clearly defines the Ugandan courts as the only branch of the state to hold judicial powers. Article 128 unambiguously guarantees the independence of the judiciary; from external interference.

In concluding the discussion, on the subject, this chapter has sought to demonstrate that the separation of powers is very important for any country. This is because it ensures, among other things, that the rights of people are best secured by a written constitution; that entrenches fundamental human rights and freedoms and is enforced by a judiciary composed of men and women of learning and integrity. The discussion has brought to the fore, the inescapable fact that, in the course of executing their constitutional mandate, there is bound, on occasion, to be friction and tension amongst the three organs of the state; but that, when such tensions arise, they must be addressed soberly and mutually; so that the great prize that the constitution sought to secure for everybody, namely liberty, does not become a casualty.

The chapter has also shown that there is no universal model of separation of powers, no absolute separation of powers and also that most constitutions tend to reflect a separation of powers that is consistent with their history and circumstances. Lastly, this chapter has endeavored to show that any model of separation of powers must allow for checks and balances that impose restraints by one organ over another to ensure accountability. It is hoped that the discussion has made it very clear, both to the schooled and unschooled in legal matters, that an essential component of the doctrine of separation of powers doctrine is that of an independent judiciary; which functions freely, without interference from the other branches of the state.

Chapter Four

DEFERENCE OR SUBMISSION?

The preceding chapter introduced the doctrine of separation of powers; and pointed out its essential features. However, the discussion was by no means exhaustive; and this chapter extends the discussion of this important topic. The starting point, in the extrapolation, is that any discussion on the separation of powers raises the important question of when the judiciary should defer to the other organs of the state. This can be a very delicate matter to deal with; as the discussion in this chapter will show. For the sake of clarity, it is important to mention that the term 'deference', as it used in this chapter, does not mean submissiveness. It simply involves the principle that the courts, out of respect for the legislature, executive and other agencies of government, may decline to make their own independent judgment on a particular case.

The rationale for judicial deference may be premised on the need to respect the separation of powers; or the need to recognize that when an administrative agency, which is empowered to do so, makes a decision, that agency is best placed, in terms of know -how or expertise, to make certain determinations in taking that decision. However, deference recognizes that even polycentric decisions are challengeable; on the basis that they may violate the constitution. With respect to the executive, it is often said that it is not the task of the judiciary to usurp the functions of the executive; by substituting its decisions for the judiciary's authority, as charged, by law, to decide on the matters in question.

Any discussion on the issue of deference must point out that it applies in different contexts and situations. There is deference which is based on fact finding by parliament, or any of its committees. There is that which is based on an administrative agency's superior technical competence; and deference to special governmental institutions such as a Military Council or Tribunal; or such similar bodies. Generally speaking, it is considered that judicial functions simply do not lend themselves to the kinds of factual enquiries, cost-benefit analyses, political compromises, implementation strategies and budgetary priority decisions which are normally the province of the executive. It is, therefore, correct to assert that 'deference' is an attitude, of the court, regarding the boundaries of separation of powers. It does not mean that courts are subservient to the other arms of the state, or, indeed, that they must show blind reverence to their interpretations of the law. Rather, deference imports respect for the decision-making process of adjudicative bodies; with regard to both the facts and the law. Deference is, therefore, a mechanism of respecting the separation of powers and ensuring that government functions smoothly.

Every constitution sets out, in varying degrees of precision, the powers of the three branches of the government. In some countries, there is no mention of the separation of powers in explicit terms. The same is implied from the structure of the constitution. In modern times, there is talk of the fourth arm of the state; which refers to a raft of constitutional bodies; such as human rights commissions, gender commissions, office of the public protector, auditor general, equality opportunities commissions and anti-corruption bodies. This fourth estate consists of bodies that are intended to promote good governance.

The principle of mutual respect is a central characteristic feature of the separation of powers. What often undermines the principle of mutual respect is a weak constitutional foundation and culture. In most African countries, executives wield more power, and influence, by virtue of their control of resources. This often undermines the idea of a proper separation of powers characterized by mutual respect. As a result, deference is too frequently seen as a quality which only the courts owe to parliament and cabinet and which the latter are not expected to reciprocate; and likewise between themselves. This sometimes leads to the notion that 'deference' is submission; an approach which is hardly conducive to democratic accountability and responsiveness.

The precise boundaries of separation of powers are a matter for the courts to determine. They may be context specific, may vary from case to case and may even shift, over time. The boundaries may also be in response to real, or perceived, levels of democratic responsiveness to the electorate. Courts, all over the globe, differ in terms of the level of scrutiny that they bring to bear on any issue that serves before them for judicial review. Some courts tend to engage in strict scrutiny, while others do not. What is important is that, in determining the boundaries on separation of powers, the judiciary must not pay lip service to the effect of the bill of rights, rationality and legality; as constraining and/or controlling factors.

In order to properly exercise their powers, which include the power to determine the boundaries of each other's sphere of influence, the courts must be independent and impartial. The judiciary must carry out this task with integrity and sensitivity. Given the fact that it has the final word on the boundaries of each branch, the judiciary is, clearly, in a privileged position; since the other branches have no such power; and are only expected to respect the pronouncement of the judiciary; even when they may be unhappy with such determination. This privileged position places an obligation on the courts to go about this assignment with modesty and humility; and to be willing to be held accountable for their conduct, both within and outside court.

In many modern constitutions, there are two areas of modern governance which throw the separation of powers, and the role of the judiciary, in a democracy, into sharp relief. The first is a fast-developing tool in the hands of any judiciary, and it concerns its authority to review the regularity, and even the reasonableness, of administrative and, sometimes executive, action or conduct. The second area is the growing tendency to expect modern constitutions, either expressly or impliedly, to guarantee a minimal level of the provision of social services by government; in the form of socio-economic rights. Each of these will be dealt with summarily below.

It is often said that cases of high national policy are not appropriate for judicial review. The examples of high national policy are many; but a good one may be a decision, by government, to deploy a section of the national army for peace keeping in some other countries. Another example may be the dismissal of a state minister from cabinet. Courts dealing with constitutional cases of high national importance often find themselves caught up between a rock and a hard place; as they have to make deference determinations. These are decisions with respect to the power and authority of another branch of the state; which compel them to dispense with certain issues serving before them.

It is interesting that lawyers, judges and politicians often talk of separation of powers in general terms, but they hardly interrogate the question that often bothers judges, namely when the courts should defer to the executive or the legislature. One of the characteristics of deference is that it may either be appropriate, or in appropriate. It is appropriate where the matter before the court can be best resolved by the other arms of the state. Stretching the subject a little further, it is somewhat intriguing that while deference has been examined in various contexts, more especially in the context of administrative law, it has never been analyzed rigorously and deeply; as a fundamental issue for constitutional jurisprudence, particularly in so far as it relates to human rights. When all is said and done, the plain fact remains that despite the profound effects, and the wide scope of deference in modern judicial review, the concept remains malleable, indeterminate and not well defined. As a result, it continues to be practiced in some jurisdictions, and with disturbing frequency, in cases involving fundamental constitutional rights.

The most problematic examples of judicial review are those in which litigants pray that a law enacted by a democratically elected parliament be declared unconstitutional. This kind of relief brings, into sharp focus, possible tension and even conflict between the judiciary and the elected representatives of the people. Quite often, the dilemma is whether, or not, to defer to parliament. In some instances, and for the sake of upholding the values of the constitution, judicial restraint may require deference, in consequence of which the law is sustained. However, an activist court may be less restrained and may, in consequence, invalidate the law sought to be impugned.

There are two examples, in South Africa, which illustrate the tension that judicial review can cause between the judiciary and the executive. In the 1897 case of Brown v Leyds, then Chief Justice Kotzé held that the informal laws passed, without notice, by a simple majority vote, were invalid on the ground of incompatibility with the Constitution. He further held that sovereignty vested in the people of the Republic and not in the Volksraand (the South African Parliament at that time); that the constitution created fundamental law with which parliament was obliged to conform; and that it was the duty of the court to declare invalid; any measures which were not in conformity with the Constitution. President's Kruger's reaction to this decision was to pass a bill, through the Volksraand, denying the constitutional competence of the judiciary to exercise the testing right and, instead, empowering the President to dismiss any judge who failed to assure him that he would not exercise the 'so-called right of testing.' Ultimately, and in consequence of the tension sparked by the case, the President dismissed the Chief Justice.

The second example of the tension that can ensue between the judiciary and the executive, as a result of judicial review, is the South African case of Harris v Minister of the Interior; where the court invalidated legislation which disenfranchised coloured voters. The government's response to the judgment was to pass, again by the ordinary bicameral method, the High Court of Parliament Act; which provided that any judgment of the Appellate Division, invalidating an Act of Parliament, was to be reviewed by Parliament itself, sitting as a High Court of Parliament. After the High Court had set aside the decision in the Vote case, the High Court of Parliament was, itself, struck down by the Appellate Division in Minister of the Interior v Harris (the High Court of Parliament case). It was held that the High Court of Parliament was not a court.

Having discussed the issue of deference of the organs of the state, and in particular the judiciary and the executive, with some depth, a key issue that arises is the imperative for a coherent methodology. One may ask why the need for this. A starting point would be that a general survey of the case law, on cases in which the courts debated whether or not to defer to the legislature or other agencies, suggests one general malady; namely the absence of a coherent methodology that can ensure certainty in the law. Most deference determinations, emanating from the apex courts, lack intellectual rigour and thoroughness and the attendant legal uncertainty, arising from the absence of a coherent methodology. This leaves the lower courts confused as to how to approach issues of deference. The end result, which is not in the interest of constitutional law, is a muddled up body of constitutional law; which leaves the choice of which case law to follow, on deference, to individual judges or courts.

It is suggested that the courts could improve the consistency, and intellectual rigour, of their deference determinations by developing a broad set of factors that guide the courts as to when to defer and when not to defer. The common reason that is often given by the courts, for choosing to defer, is that they may not be as knowledgeable, about a particular subject matter, as the specific agency of government that is mandated to deal with it. While they could well be plausible, these criteria may need to be developed further. This is because it is common cause, in many jurisdictions, that the extent to which government agencies defer, with respect to the requisite know-how on how to deal with a particular case, varies from one case to another; depending on who, within the agency, is taking the decision; and how well placed they are, to execute that decision. Similarly, the courts' capacity to review decisions may also differ considerably. It is suggested that the decision to defer or not to defer must not be a function of stereotypes;

but rather, it must be an assessment of each state organ's strengths and weaknesses; relative to the issue that falls for determination.

In many jurisdictions, parliaments use the separation of powers argument to ask the courts to back off from reviewing any so called 'high policy' matters; and in many instances they succeed in scaring the courts off. It is generally accepted that there may be cases where it is appropriate for the courts to defer to parliament. However, where parliament's proceedings are, otherwise, a mockery of due process in that they plainly trample upon human rights, and there is total absence of good faith in the manner in which parliament is considering a particular issue that is serving before it, then it would, most certainly, be inappropriate for a court to accept the invitation to back off. For instance, where there is a clear disconnect between parliament's findings and the evidence on record, the court would be failing in its duty to quash the decision simply because of bald separation of powers arguments.

Other than parliaments, a number of government agencies such as the army, prison authorities and other specialized agencies often claim that the courts must defer to them. The reason that is often cited, for insisting on deference, is that it is the administrative agencies' subject matter expertise that is at play. Unlike parliaments, government agencies often administer policy within a limited area; and employ expert professional staff. For instance, a question may arise as to whether a prisoner's request to attend a parent's funeral ought to be granted or, even more fundamentally, whether a prisoner ought to be allowed to marry while serving out a sentence. Indeed, it is often emphasized that agencies exist because they are institutionally well suited to deal with certain unique questions; that are consistent with their narrow mandate. A close scrutiny of deference, based on the above reasons, seems theoretically incoherent in some respects. It is also said that where a matter involves budgetary considerations, the court must be slow to intervene because they are less knowledgeable about resource allocations.

Another area in which the courts are often asked to back off is on matters touching, or related to, national security or international relations; ostensibly because the issues are often 'sensitive' and meriting special concessions. The courts' perceived relative inferior knowledge on matters of national security and international relations is, invariably, cited as reason enough why they should not 'second guess' the decisions of the special governmental agencies which are mandated to deal with the specific issues that arise. Unfortunately, the courts often, uncritically, accept to have their jurisdiction ousted by mere assertions that they lack requisite expertise. It does not help that the courts hardly attempt to examine the basis of the alleged 'sensitivity'; which can always be done in camera if need be. It is a different matter where governments can demonstrate sound basis for their concern that the court should not exercise jurisdiction over a matter. Where this happens, it is then up to the court to strike a proper balance relative to other considerations that may be implicated.

It has already been stated, and it true, that courts may not always strike a perfect balance. However, the courts must always rigorously scrutinize the specific institution and the circumstances of each case. The reason for a careful scrutiny arises from the very nature of a constitution containing a bill of rights. As has also been already indicated, a constitution, by its nature, contains multiple, and at times contradictory, values. The courts usually resolve these contradictions by concluding that one value trumps another.

One other reason that is often invoked by governments, in their efforts to keep courts away from scrutinizing their decisions, in particular those which touch on national security, is the separation of powers argument. Governments often argue that the constitution expressly confers the executive with the authority to deal with matters of national security. More often than not, it is suggested that the military is a separate community; which is subject to different rules from those that govern the broader society. However, and no matter how complicated a national security argument may be, the courts musts stay true to their constitutional mandate. Adjudicators should know that far from constitutional overreaching, deference determinations, in a constitutional democracy, are given; and arise from time to time. A cardinal point to remember is that in any democratic state, legal controversies must be resolved in factual contexts. The courts must always insist on proof of facts; that justify a particular cause of action; which may be the cause of a dispute serving before them.

With respect to international relations, it is often said that the fluidity of world events, perhaps, justifies permitting governments to have the last word on certain issues; without the courts insisting that certain specific facts be proven. To this extent, the executive has often appropriated to itself overboard powers to deal with the threat of terrorism; and has asked the courts not to interfere. For instance, some governments have sought to carry out detentions for prolonged periods of time; where the suspicions related to involvement in terrorism. This is where judicial review becomes a very handy tool in providing checks and balances, among the traditional three arms of government, in order to uphold the separation of powers. By way of explanation, judicial review is the power of the courts to subject public power, whether by the legislature or the executive, to judicial scrutiny for compliance with the law, and to give appropriate relief. This particular power of the courts has grown, phenomenally, and I might add of necessity, in recent years. Opponents of judicial review argue that it diverts and undermines democracy. The judiciary's common response to this criticism is to exercise self-restraint; and defer to the legislature when evaluating the human rights pedigree of legislation. As was earlier stated the judiciary, just like other state organs, is duty bound to stay within its lane on the separation of powers highway. It, too, should not exceed its limits; save to the extent that it is righting a wrong committed by another state organ; such as when it pronounces a piece of legislation to be unconstitutional. But even in the exercise of this function, the judiciary must be alive to the fact that there are times when it needs to defer to the legislature.

It is noteworthy that, over the years, the relationship between the three branches of government, with respect to human rights, has been evolving towards a modern constitutionalism; which rejects the old dichotomy between political and legal constitutionalism, and embraces the shared responsibility of all branches of the state, the government, parliament and the courts; in order to uphold the rule of law. This dialogic model of constitutionalism views the judiciary, and the legislature, as partners in a common enterprise, rather than adversaries in a perpetual contest for supremacy. This progressive constitutional dialogue model has developed, in a number of jurisdictions, against the backdrop of a changing human rights landscape. The changes include the creation of parliamentary select committees to strengthen the role of parliaments, in protecting human rights, and also to improve the quality of legislative deliberation on rights. These changes are critical towards creating and maintaining a culture of justification, whereby citizens can reasonably expect that every exercise of power will be justified, and that 'the leadership' given by government rests on the cogency of the case offered in defence of its decisions; and not the fear inspired by force at its command'.

Although the general idea is that every exercise of public power must be justifiable and based on facts and reason, the courts have not adopted a uniform approach to the circumstances under which they would set aside a decision that, ordinarily, is considered to be the province of the executive; such as a case dealing with allocation of resources. As a general rule, the courts are reluctant to super -impose their decisions with respect to such matters. Some courts have insisted that unless the applicant/ litigant is able to establish bad faith, mala-fide or that the decision is, in all the circumstances, so grossly perverse or unreasonable; that no reasonable authority could have come to it, the judiciary should be slow to disturb it.

Generally, the courts have tended to tread with extreme caution with respect to matters concerning the distribution of resources. This is because of the general belief that the executive is best suited to do so; and that the principle of separation of powers allocates the task of resource allocation to the executive branch of government; and not to the judiciary and, as such, it is the court's duty to recognize the constitutional importance of executive freedom, within limits, to distribute resources.

In a constitutional democracy, such as obtains in Botswana, characterised as it is by loose separation of powers, deference is often necessary. However, deference, if not properly exercised, could result in the fundamental rights of individuals being curtailed by a bureaucratic state, and its agencies. This would necessitate judicial review; which is an instrument devised to prevent legality and the rule of law from being blunted and rendered ineffectual. Speaking for myself, and I daresay a few others, judicial review is a necessary check on the decisions of the bureaucratic state; and its agencies to ensure that they are lawful.

In the field of Administrative Law, it has been suggested that judicial deference is particularly appropriate where the subject matter of an administrative action is very technical; or of a kind in which a court has no particular proficiency. The courts and lawyers cannot pretend, or at least be expected, to have the skills of economists, scientists, or any field of expertise. For example, in the case of Secretary of State for the Home Office v Rehman, the House of Lords were reviewing a decision, by the Home Secretary, to deport a Pakistani national on the grounds of national security. The courts held that the executive was the best judge of the need for international co-operation to combat terrorism; and to develop counter terrorist strategies, since they had access to special information and expertise in security matters.

In another case, that of Sauve v Canada *(No 2)*, the court proposed a deferential approach where inmates were challenging their limit on the right to vote. The court held that it owed deference to parliament; because the matter was dealing with philosophical and political considerations. The appellate court, however, had a different view, which was that the right to vote was fundamental to democracy and the rule of law; and could not be lightly set aside. The court reasoned that the limits on the right to vote required not deference, but careful examination.

In yet another case, namely, Doctors for Life International v Speaker of the National Assembly, the South African court was faced with the question of whether it was competent, for the court, to grant a declaratory relief to the effect that parliament had failed to comply with its constitutional obligation to facilitate public involvement in the legislative process. The court held that there was no express constitutional provision that precluded it (the court) from doing so. On the one hand, the case raised the question of the court's competence to interfere with the autonomy of parliament to regulate its internal proceedings and, on the other, it raised the question of the duty of the court to enforce the constitution and, in particular, to ensure that the law making process conformed to the constitution.

The courts in other jurisdictions, notably in the Commonwealth, have been quite cautious when it comes to issues touching on separation of powers. No court would want to trespass into the province of the other branch of government. At the same time, courts are very careful not to abdicate their responsibilities. In consequence of this sense of responsibility, they have claimed the right, as well as the duty, to intervene; in order to prevent the violation of the constitution.

As has already been pointed out, deference may be both appropriate and inappropriate, depending on the circumstances under which it is invoked. Deference may be appropriate for a decision involving competing social and political policies. In cases involving the alleged violation of fundamental human rights, deference may not be appropriate. This is because human rights are fundamental to our democracy, and the rule of law, and cannot be lightly set aside. A law suit which is based on the alleged violation of a right does not require deference, but careful examination. When determining such cases, the courts are faced with the reality that it is not a matter of their substituting their philosophical preference for that of the legislature; but, rather, of ensuring that the legislature's proffered justification is supported by logic and common sense. It is important to emphasize that fundamental human rights, and freedoms, do not constitute a bucket of options; from which parliament may pick and choose at its discretion.

Deference is, similarly, not appropriate in a decision to limit fundamental rights. Human rights and freedoms are not a matter of privilege; they are inherent in every person and every government is obligated to respect, protect and fulfil them. When such rights are violated and threatened, it is the duty of the courts to ensure that same are enforced.

Having regard to the above narrative, the following guidelines on deference become apparent:

> Greater deference will be due where the subject matter is peculiarly within the constitutional responsibility of democratic government; such as the defence of the realm of immigration control, and less when it lies within the constitutional responsibility of the court; such as in the field of criminal justice;

> Greater deference is due where the subject matter lies more readily within the actual or potential expertise of the democratic powers; such as governmental decisions in the area of macro-economic policy;

> There is more scope for deference where the constitution, itself, requires a balance to be struck;

and much less so where rights are expressed in unqualified terms;

The nature of the right, e.g. whether the right in question is unqualified or qualified determines the level of deference to be attached; as does the extent to which the issue involves consideration of social, economic or political factors;

Another determinant of deference is whether the rights claimed have a high degree of constitutional protection e.g. political speech, access to the court or intimate aspects of private life.

In summation, the view I take is that the responsibility thrust on the courts, by constitutions, in countries where the constitution is supreme, can be more readily achieved by:

an acceptance that the constitution, by definition, mandates a principle of strict scrutiny where it is alleged that constitutional rights have been breached;

a recognition that the courts, themselves, have a legitimate democratic role in subjecting governmental decision making to close analysis;

a recognition that it will often be necessary for a court to defer to the judgment of others; but that the critical issue is to evaluate how much deference is due to that judgment, in a particular case which is being decided.

At the end of the day, I am able to assert, without fear of contradiction, that judicial review which ultimately leads to the court setting aside laws passed by the legislature, for want of compliance with the constitution, does not amount to a subversion of democracy. This is so because the power to do so resides in the constitution being the supreme law of the land. In saying all this, I am not suggesting that the courts have the power to meddle in politics or, indeed, to usurp the functions of the executive to formulate policy. What I am merely saying is that the courts have the power to adjudicate upon questions of whether the policies which are passed by the executive, on their implementation, result in the violation of fundamental human rights. If the laws passed by the legislature, and the policies formulated by the executive violate the constitution, then the courts must so declare; without blinking.

In this chapter, which has focused on the issue of deference, it has been sought to argue that the doctrine of separation of powers requires the three arms of the state to respect each other's boundaries of competence. It has also been pointed out that whilst the courts must defer in an appropriate case, they should not be unduly submissive. Additionally, it would be of help for the courts to lay out, or articulate, a clear and meaningful methodology of when to defer and when not to defer to the executive or the legislature. The reality, in most jurisdictions, is that the courts do not meaningfully lay out a clear methodology for determining when to defer. Quite often, deference determinations are poorly reasoned; resting less on careful considerations and relying baldly on the fact that the separation of powers doctrine prohibits the trespassing, by the organs of the state, into each other's sphere of competence. Aside this, there are times when the courts' deference determinations are not supported by any legal analysis. In closing, but by no means exhausting the discussion on deference, it has to be pointed out that judicial candour is essential; if the people are to have confidence in a judiciary's constitutional determinations.

Chapter Five

DO JUDGES MAKE LAW?

To ask the question whether judges makes law in a constitutional democracy, in the context of separation of powers and deference, as discussed in an earlier chapter, is to invite controversy. It is a question that often divides the legal fraternity, not least the judges. In this chapter, attempt is made to do two things; firstly, to discuss whether judges make law or not and, secondly, to clarify and defend the concept of judicial activism. Posing the question of whether judges make law implies that it is permissible for them to do so; and this is a question that has pre-occupied the minds of legal scholars and philosophers for centuries. Even as this question continues to be mulled over, the truth is that there are still a number of judges who detest the very idea that judges make law.

The debate as to whether judges make law is centuries old. Many years ago, two prominent legal jurists pronounced themselves on this question. The renowned philosopher, Jeremy Bentham, considered it, 'childish fiction' that judges do not make law. Lord Reid, a renowned British Judge, considered the view that judges do not make law as a 'fairy tale'. He stated that:

"There was a time when it was thought almost indecent to suggest that judges make law – they only declare it. Those with a taste for fairy tales seem to have thought that in some

Aladdin's cave there is hidden the Common Law in all its splendour and that on a judge's appointment, there descends on him knowledge of the magic words Open Sesame. Bad decisions are given when the judge has muddled the pass word and the wrong door opens. But we do not believe in fairy tales anymore."

Centuries ago, way back in 1345, an English lawyer is reported to have argued before a panel of judges: "I think you will do as others have done in the same case, or else we do not know what the law is". "It is the will of the Justices', responded Judge Hillary. Chief Justice Stonore intervened: "No, law is that which is right".

It is very interesting that the above exchange, which took place in 1345, is still with us in the 21st century; and I imagine it is bound to be alive for a long time to come. A progressive development, in this debate, is that slowly, and incrementally, concessions are being made, albeit begrudgingly, that judges do, indeed, make law in their own unique way. It is perhaps correct to assert that in this present age, no reasonably informed lawyer would contest the view, which is fast gaining traction, that judges do make law.

Judges are, of course, not primary law givers. The primary law makers, in most democracies, are the legislatures. Having explained that judges are not the primary law makers, it would be helpful to say in what way judges make law. Generally, the courts operate on the basis of precedents.

These bind the lower courts; where the facts and the law, to be applied, are similar to the ones on which the higher courts have already pronounced the law. Having touched on the issue of precedents, it becomes imperative to define what is meant by that term. A basic definition is that precedents are legal principles developed by the courts, from time to time, when dealing with various controversies of human existence.

Precedents help in ensuring that the law is predictable and certain; and that lawyers are best able to advise their clients on what the position of the law is. I hasten to add that precedents are not cast in stone and, as society evolves, they often change. It could be said, without any fear of contradiction, that when judges develop precedents, or when they abandon a particular precedent on the basis that it is not good law, and then go on to develop new legal principles, they are, in fact, making law. Many of those that are schooled in common law traditions will know that the common law is made by judges. It is, therefore, within the province of the courts to determine when precedents can be amended, modified or abolished.

It is often said that judicial activists do not appreciate the value of precedent. This cannot be correct. Judicial activists appreciate the value of precedent; but caution against slavish adherence to it, even when the facts and circumstances have changed, or a grave injustice would result from mechanical adherence to precedent. Judicial activists acknowledge that, as a general rule, precedent is an effective safeguard against arbitrary, whimsical, capricious, unpredictable and autocratic decision making. It prevents the citizen from being at the mercy of an individual mind that is uncontrolled by due process of law. Despite this, however, it must also be recognized that the application of known legal principles will not always be possible. Sometimes, novel situations arise, to which the known principles cannot be applied; and we then need theories for deciding whether an existing authority is to be applied, distinguished or overruled.

Judicial activists acknowledge that reliance on precedent is not always possible, or even desirable. Changes in social or political conditions sometimes require new law, and old principles may simply be entirely inappropriate for circumstances not previously contemplated. For instance, a present day court may have to consider and evaluate evidence relating to the contents of electronic mail (e-mail) exchanged between persons. Quite obviously, this is a consideration which a court of yesteryear would not have had to deal with; for the simple reason that the technology concerning electronic mail had not yet been developed. Consequently, reliance on a precedent for a case involving a handwritten letter would not serve much purpose with regard to a case involving an e-mail; because that level of technological advancement, in communication was not something previously contemplated.

It cannot be contested that the courts continuously develop law, whether it be the common law or statutory law and, in doing so, they often disregard precedent that is archaic. Where the law is vague, the court may, in interpreting it, create a new principle, which becomes part of the law. Viewed from this vantage point, it could be said that in the course of interpretation, judges make law. It is also the mandate of the courts to interpret the constitution. In relation to other laws, constitutions tend to be shorter, and couched in elastic terms, so as to provide for the aspirations of generations yet to be born. By their very nature, constitutions call for interpretation from time to time. This is perhaps even more so than for ordinary pieces of legislation, which tend to be elaborate and to focus on fewer areas than the constitution; on account that the constitution is supposed to be all encompassing. It is, therefore, inescapable that judges would be required, periodically, to reform the law in the interest of clarity, efficiency and fairness.

Continuing with the question of whether judges make law, the idea or the notion that they do so is frowned upon by many politicians. As a result of this, tension between the judiciary and the legislature is fast escalating; particularly in those countries where the courts are increasingly keen to review the exercise of public power. Be that as it may, the stark reality is that we live in a world where the courts are increasingly mandated to police the exercise of public power, in order to keep it within the limits of rationality, reasonableness, fairness and proportionality. Consequently, a case can, and must be, made for judicial activism.

Although the question as to whether, or not, judges make law has existed for centuries, it was not until the 1940's that some scholarship on the matter began to emerge. Arthur Schlesinger coined the term *'judicial activism'* in 1947; in an article that appeared in the 'Fortune' magazine. Schlesinger's article profiled all the nine US Supreme Court justices who were serving, as such, at that time; and explained the alliances and divisions among them. The article characterized Justices Black, Douglas, Murphy, and Rutlege as the *Judicial Activists*' and Justices Frankfurter, Jackson, and Burton as the '*Champions of Self Restraint*'. Justice Reed and Chief Justice Vinson comprised a middle group. According to Schlesinger, judicial activists believe that law and politics are inseparable. They see judicial decisions as 'result-oriented', because no result is fore-ordained. They also adopt the famous 'Learned Hand' dictum that "the words a judge must construe are empty vessels into which he can pour nearly anything he will."

In contrast to 'judicial activists' as defined by Schlesinger, the judges who subscribe to judicial restraint begin to look like timorous souls; who are all too willing to abdicate judicial responsibility in order to maintain a status quo that may not be fair or just. Schlesinger writes that judicial activists believe that courts cannot escape politics and it is, therefore, up to them to use its political power for wholesome social purposes. Schlesinger explains that the champions of self -restraint, on the other hand, are more skeptical of individual judges' notions of justice. To them, laws have fixed meanings, and deviation from those meanings is inappropriate; no matter which groups may benefit from the departure.

Schlesinger mentions another school of thought, the Frankfurter-Jackson school, which apparently seeks to resist judicial supremacy, or law making by judges, either of the right or of the left, in the name of deference to the legislative will, and the need to protect the separation of powers and the democratic process. According to the Frankfurter-Jackson school, if the legislature makes mistakes, it is up to the legislature, itself, to remedy them, and not the courts. Frankfurter-Jackson scholars contend that any other course would denude democracy of its meaning, and unnecessarily catapult the judiciary into a law-making arm of the state, just like the legislature, and that would, undoubtedly, be inappropriate. According to this school of thought, the law, that is to say, common law, statutes, and the constitution, are not 'empty vessels'. The Frankfurter-Jackson school of thought contends that to allow judges a free hand, when interpreting the law, may lead to judicial despotism.

A characteristic of judicial activism which is well worth noting is that, as a concept, it tends to be over simplified; or even understood in a crude fashion. However, when properly understood, judicial activism can represent a number of distinct jurisprudential ideas that are worthy of further investigation. When it is contended, as is usually the case, that striking down arguably constitutional actions of other branches of government is judicial activism, that invites debate over the age-old questions, firstly, of how one can best interpret the constitution, and, secondly, what should be the proper scope of judicial review in a constitutional democracy.

The other notable thing about judicial activism is that a charge, which is often laid against it, is that by disregarding precedent, judges undermine the law. The issue of disregarding precedent is a complex one; in that it raises issues about the nature of judicial functions and the amount of deference owed to different types of precedent. These are questions which are as important as they are difficult to resolve.

It is indisputable that, over the years, the term judicial activism has acquired so many distinct, and even contradictory, meanings. Nevertheless, when explained carefully, the term can be a starting point for meaningful conversation about the dynamism of a judge's work. In ordinary debates that take place in the streets, and sometimes even in the hallowed halls of the judiciary, judicial activism generally has a negative connotation. It is usually understood, or taken, to mean judges who are perceived to have a political agenda, or are too liberal and too quick to impose their political views on society. Critics of judicial activism argue that if the activist judge is making decisions spurred on by what he, or she, believes in, then the courts become unpredictable; and justice is almost at the mercy of a whim.

Opponents of judicial activism argue that a bill of rights does *not* provide justification for the courts to disregard any legal rule; whether it is statutory or common-law. Some extremists even equate judicial activism to the notion of the dictatorship of the proletariat; calling it '*the dictatorship of the wig and gown*'. However, according to Justice Harms, this so-called 'dictatorship of the wig and gown' not only defeats the spirit, and content, of the constitution and goes beyond the scope of the law; but it also blurs the boundaries of separation of powers.

The flip side of the extremist view is the argument that contrary to the impaired, and negative understanding of what judicial activism entails, the judges who are regarded as judicial activists, today, are generally those who are progressive; and have the courage, and intellectual gravitas, to appreciate constitutional values. It is very important in any discussion on this subject, to emphasize that *'judicial activism'* does not mean the same thing as *'judicial adventurism'*. These are two very different concepts; because the latter is a consequence of a judge merely plodding through the law, without putting forth any intellectually persuasive reasoning; as a basis of making a decision in a particular manner.

As I discuss judicial activism, I endeavour to demonstrate that negative criticism of judicial activism does not resonate with my understanding of the term. A question may be posed as to why I take this view. My brief response would be that I am inclined to that mindset because, generally speaking, judges should be servants of the law and, as such, they should not be at liberty to depart from it capriciously, or maneuver their way around the law in order to give effect to their personal positions. However, and as has already been stated earlier, the law is a complicated subject. It is not an exact science, if at all it can be considered as such. This assertion, therefore, suggests that judges may differ in their interpretation of the law; with some interpreting the law narrowly and others doing so expansively. In reality, however, the consequences of permitting such an elastic manner of interpreting the law could have wide ranging implications.

Returning to the subject under scrutiny, I emphatically state that, in my mind, judicial activism does not mean judicial lawlessness. Instead, it is the willingness to interpret the law, where interpretation is required, in a way that is consistent with the values of human rights, democracy and the rule of law. After all, judges are not mathematical calculators or robots; but juridical scientists who must interpret the law in such a way as to serve the ends of justice. To this end, they can, within limits, develop the law to keep pace with the needs and aspirations of the contemporary society.

A survey of contemporary literature and jurisprudence suggests that activism, in the manner in which I have suggested it, is common in the field of human rights; and not necessarily in the area of political and social reforms. Be that as it may, it must always be understood that in a constitutional democracy, where the supreme law of the land is the constitution, sovereignty lies with the people; and the courts only exercise a delegated authority assigned to them by the people. As a result, when they are interpreting the constitution, the courts should always seek to advance the will of the people, as captured in the constitution, and not their will. Apart from this important duty that they owe to the people, it is important to always bear in mind that the courts are institutions which belong to the people, and that the judges exercise their judicial powers for the benefit of people. They have an obligation to ensure that the constitution, which they are entrusted to uphold, remains, at all times, relevant to the lives of the people. When the courts fail to carry out this duty, then there can be no constitutional democracy to speak of.

There is an unmistakable trend, throughout the common law world, towards increased judicial intervention. The courts are the creation of the people; and are established to serve their communities independently, competently and impartially. Judges are expected to use their learning, knowledge of the law and professional ethos, to do justice according to law. They should not hesitate to respond to the needs of the individual members of society and should, if need be, interpret the law in a manner that achieves justice.

In a constitutional democracy all three arms of government derive their legitimacy from the constitution; which also delineates the individual functions of the arms of government. The constitution empowers the judiciary to interpret it (constitution) and to review the actions and policies of the other branches of government; for the benefit of the people. Bearing in mind the evolving nature of society, it would be retrogressive to condemn the constitution to a static document which does not change with time; and it is from this perspective that judicial activism should be perceived.

The most common accusation regarding judicial activism is that judges impose their own views on society; with regard to what the concept of justice entails. This charge is not an entirely merited criticism. No judge can view, or interpret, the constitution with the mind of any person; other than his or her own. It follows, therefore, that the argument that judges impose their own views on the concept of justice is not particularly helpful. It is a fact that judges are professionals. They have been trained in the law; and it is their training that helps them to navigate complex legal and factual controversies. Of course, no one can pretend that in the course of interpreting the law, judges do not bring their own experiences to bear. The primary issue should be whether they impose views contrary to the spirit and letter of the constitution; and not whether they impose their own views about justice. This is because few judges would deliberately depart from the spirit of the constitution to impose their personal preference as to the meaning of justice.

It is axiomatic that the idea that each of the three branches of the state would be accessible to those governed, on a somewhat equal basis, is implicit in the doctrine of separation of powers. That doctrine, as has been explained, draws its mandate from the broad scheme of constitutions; which subscribe to the values of democracy and the rule of law. However, the general trend across most democracies is the alienation of the people; and absence of adequate access to the executive and legislature, in particular. It is on account of this lack of access that, increasingly, individuals, civil society organizations and political parties are using the courts to hold both the executive and parliament accountable. For instance, those charged with criminal offences, victims of violence, those who are unfairly dismissed from employment, those who are unfairly demoted and those who are unfairly excluded from the electoral process are generally powerless, when it comes to influencing the executive and the legislature. So, on many occasions, these people trust the courts to foster an inclusive society; limited as it may seem.

Having looked at the commonest accusation with regard to judicial activism, it is only right to point out one of the strongest points in its favour. To wit, the inability of the legislature and parliament to protect the rights of individuals, often on the basis of political expediency, is one of the strongest reasons why judicial activism should be celebrated; and not demonized. A rigid conceptualization of the doctrine of separation of powers, that seeks to ask the courts to unduly defer to the other branches of government, even where the decision sought to be challenged infringes the constitution, makes little sense to the notion that the courts are the custodians of the rule of law. It, equally, does not make sense to those that are excluded from the political process. For such people, the courts are the forum of last resort; and the argument that the courts are counter majoritarian offers no help to them.

While it cannot be denied that it has a hold in some segments of society, the argument that the courts are counter majoritarian, or are otherwise undemocratic, is flawed; because it uncritically assumes that other branches of the state are democratic. This assumption could not be more unjustifiable. It cannot be taken that the legislature is more democratic, than the other arms of government, simply because it is elected periodically; say once every four or five years. That would be a very weak democracy; as it would lack other requirements such as a participatory, responsive and accountable legislature or executive.

The critical need for the protection of human rights has been brought up several times in the preceding chapters of this book; along with role that the judiciary is expected to play in that regard. However, in evaluating the ability of other branches to protect the rights of everyone, it is also important to have regard to how resources may serve to distort a democratic dispensation. It can hardly be contested that those with the resources have a disproportionate influence in determining who gets elected, and who ultimately gets appointed to the executive. The importance of resources is glaringly evident from the fact that the lack, thereof, excludes a large number of otherwise competent, and visionary, members of the populace from considering being elected to political office. For this reason, the charge that it is a rich person's game cannot be dismissed lightly. In fact, this claim is given even more credence by the fact that those, within the legislative process, who sponsored candidates and political parties, often have an upper hand and influence, both visibly and invisibly, in the way a country is being run.

Turning to the executive, its democratic credentials are also not beyond credible criticism. In some countries, dominant parties practically impose their leaders on the people; since those leaders would not have been subjected to direct election by the people. Furthermore, the implementing arm of the executive often comprises life time civil servants; who are not accountable to the people. In essence, in the contemporary society, which is characterized by alienation of many people and interest groups from the political process, judicial activism serves a functional role. It is a safety net which ensures that governmental power, or decision making, is justifiable, reasonable and rational; and that it serves a legitimate government purpose. Judicial activism must, of necessity, ensure that the people have access to their government. To this extent, it is not sufficient that legislative and executive officials are theoretically accessible; they must be actually accessible.

It cannot be argued, at least by any reasonable standards, that the courts do not serve a legitimate purpose in society. A favourable decision, by the courts, confers legitimacy to the complaints of often powerless litigants who, in the ordinary course of events, would be ignored by the other branches of government. It is a notorious fact, in some democracies, that approaching members of the executive or legislature with a complaint, concerning the violation one's rights does not usually yield satisfactory results. There is generally no complaints procedure with respect to the executive and legislature and, where a complaint is filed, one is lucky to receive a response. The observation that one is lucky to get a response from the executive, where sometimes even a polite rejection is hard to come by, does not suggest that the courts are perfect. To the contrary, there are numerous complaints in respect of which the courts are quite often inaccessible to the people whom they are supposed to serve. This is on account of financial impediments, the use of technical language and even archaic laws of procedure and evidence; which are incomprehensible to ordinary litigants seeking justice from the courts. However, in comparison, to the other branches of government, the courts have a formal complaints procedure, by which they process complaints systematically.

The long and short of the discussion above is that it shows that in a world where the other arms of the state may not be sufficiently accessible, and efficient, there is a real case for judicial activism. No one disputes that judicial activism, through interpreting existing primary legislation, may generate new legal norms. That is perfectly within the province of the courts to do. However, the extolling of the benefits of judicial activism, especially in a deficient democracy, must not be misconstrued to suggest that a judge has a free hand to do what he, or she, wishes. As the famous American jurist, Cardozo, observed, a judge cannot innovate at pleasure. According to that jurist, a judge is not a knight errant; "roaming at will in pursuit of his own ideal of beauty or of goodness. He is to draw his inspiration from consecrated principles". There may be many views on Cardozo's observation; but the one thing that cannot be taken away, from it, is that it is a well- founded observation.

It having been conclusively spelled out that the courts have a critical role to play in a functional democracy, equal emphasis must be placed on the fact that the courts must not waiver in enforcing the constitutional rights of the people; and in particular those of the powerless who have no meaningful access to the other branches of government. However, the courts cannot accomplish this feat by themselves. Attorneys, as individuals and members of Bar Associations, must help the judges to come to the rescue of the powerless. In addition, to this, judges need the protection of members of the bar; especially when there is a public outrage because a judge has delivered an unpopular decision. It is not for Attorneys to also jump onto the bandwagon and criticize judges, when they, of all people, should understand that judges have a bounden duty to protect the rights of every person; even if that goes against the wishes of the majority. This being said, I hasten to add that this call to members of the bar is not to suggest that the merits of a case should not be debated; and the judge criticized if necessary. The point being made is that any criticism of a judge should be constructive; and must be done both with restraint and the necessary decorum.

As has been discussed in an earlier chapter, the courts generally operate on the principle of legal precedence; which requires that similar cases be decided in a similar manner. This promotes legal certainty, which is a fundamental requirement of the rule of law. Again, and as has already been alluded to, the essence of a precedent is that it lays down a legal principle; which is binding, especially on the lower courts. Significantly, precedents are the source of most of judge made law. In fact, the common law that is in use today evolved out of precedents.

While the lower courts are inescapably bound by legal precedents, appellate courts are free to depart from them, if it becomes necessary to do so. The effect of departure from precedent is that it may create a new legal norm, which would be binding on lower courts. It is worth noting that, occasionally, judges are asked to decide a case in which there is no precedent to guide them. In these circumstances, the judges may be said to be formulating an original precedent.

There are times when the demands of contemporary society can drive a judge to create new precedent and make new law. A document such as a constitution, that is organic, and elastic, in nature and which is meant to serve generations yet unborn, may yield a legal result which it could not have yielded decades earlier. In essence, when this new meaning is fostered on society, as a result of the changing times and society's evolution, it is not a judges' personal opinion or wish, but it is the law that speaks through the judge. This is so because the tide of history, and contemporary society, cannot be irrelevant to the function of a judge; as a professional operator. The spirit of the age cannot, and should not, leave a judge unscathed.

Every country can, perhaps, cite a judge who was pre-eminent in the development of the law to fit changed societal circumstances. In the United States, the Warren Court was considered activist and critics charged that the Chief Justice was engaged in law making. In the United Kingdom, Lord Denning has been accused of utilizing the courts as instruments of law making; especially during his tenure as Master of the Rolls in the Court of Appeal. Lord Denning is arguably the most celebrated judge that the common law jurisdictions have produced. He has been described as "England's most revolutionary judge". Clive Schmittoff wrote that "the contemporary scene in

Great Britain is unthinkable without Lord Denning. Lord Scarman characterized the post war legal order as 'the period of legal aid, reform and Lord Denning'.

True to his reputation in that regard, Lord Denning wrote that a reform minded judge is not content to accept cherished beliefs because they have long been accepted. According to Lord Denning, a reform minded judge would not follow accepted beliefs if he or she thought that to do so would occasion injustice. He reasoned that in order to do justice to the parties, such a judge would search the law for competing principles and apply the one that would best do justice to the parties.

While Lord Denning's contribution to the common law jurisprudence will always stand out, his law making approach did not go without criticism. His first major battle was with Lord Simmonds. The two disagreed, strongly, on the question of the proper approach to judicial interpretation of statutes. As a consequence of these varying approaches to statutory interpretation, Lord Denning often received strictures from the House of Lords; regarding the proper function of a judge when interpreting statutes. The celebrated judge has also been criticized for his cavalier handling of precedents; his citing authorities that did not support his preposition of the law and for glossing over inconvenient precedents.

It has to be said that Lord Denning's enthusiasm for law making, in a legal system where there is no written constitution and parliament is supreme, was daring; by all accounts. He brushed aside the usual criticism that by developing the law, he breached the doctrine of separation of powers; since the role of a judge is to interpret the law. Lord Denning also parried the common stricture that judicial law making is inherently undemocratic. For all the criticisms directed at him, few can contest the preposition that Lord Denning was one of the most innovative judges of his generation. He looked at the law as an instrument for doing justice. According to Lord Denning, justice is 'what the majority of right thinking people regard as a fair solution'.

Those of us who idolized him, during our law school days, loved Lord Denning's celebrated quotation; which served as his recurrent theme throughout his judicial life. It is a quotation of his dissenting speech in the famous case of Candler v Crane Christmas and Co. The learned judge said:

"On the one side there were the timorous souls who were fearful of allowing a new cause of action. On the other side were the bold spirits who were ready to allow it if justice required. It was fortunate for the common law that the progressives prevailed…"

It follows, from the above, that the notion that judges do not make law is both antiquated and unappealing. It is some kind of fiction. Montesquieu's theory that the judge is "no more than the mouth that produces the words of the law" is now discredited. That judges make law is clear from the development of the common law; as can be seen from the fact that the common law of today is not the same as that which existed about a hundred years ago. It keeps on developing at the instances of the judges. This applies, with equal force, to interpretation of statutory or constitutional text. Typically, in legal warfare, before a ruling a particular legal text may be assigned several meanings, but after the ruling the law is what the ruling says.

In my mind, judges must not conceal, to the public, that they make law. They must be candid and be able to explain under what circumstances they make law. Judicial power involves making binding decisions; having regard to the existing law. The existing law is a combination of legislation, constitution, common law and judicial decisions. In applying all of the above sources, in the context of the circumstances of each particular case, judges make law to a limited degree. As has already been pointed out, they are not the primary law makers, but i n today's world, where time is an essential trigger of change and a dynamic that can't be wished away, there is need to constantly develop the law so that it does not lag behind societal developments.

The moral force of any judgment, of a court, derives from the fulfilment of the judge's task of deciding a dispute by attempting fairly, and in public, to determine the truth.

Judges who insist on being absolutely passive in the courtroom and who are not committed to giving effect to the values of the constitution, but are prepared to interpret the law mechanically; even if such an approach occasions injustice do in effect, tolerate, any injustice that may result. Suffice it to say that if this was the norm, then the courts would most certainly lose the confidence of society.

Contrary to the views held by some on the subject, judicial activism does not offend the principle of separation of powers. It is the duty of the courts to say what the law is. The courts should not unduly, and unjustifiably, trespass into the lane of other arms of the state; save where the constitution gives them authority to do so. It is generally accepted that the duty of judges, which is universally accepted, is to suppress their pre-conceptions and leanings of the mind; and to make decisions based solely on the merits of each individual case. In my mind, there is merit in the view that the more acutely judges are aware of their own subconscious attitudes, the better judges they will be. They will then be able to overcome their own personal biases and prejudices, better, and make findings without being influenced by them.

Most lawyers and judges, throughout the world, would readily testify to generalized prejudice; that can occasion serious injustice if not identified and effectively suppressed. Examples that come to mind are the prejudices against women, children, diverse racial groups, refugees, the disabled and members of the Lesbian, Gay, Bisexual, Transgender and Intersex (LGBTI) community. Judges must confront their prejudices and seek to ensure that these don't influence their decisions. It is my considered view that while judges are perfectly entitled to hold personal views on any issue, they should exercise control, and discipline, over their own feelings and should always decide each case on its merits. This duty must be carried out impartially, neutrally and without regard to personal bias and prejudices or ill feelings.

Inspite of all the positives in its favour, judicial activism is often scorned because it is regarded as authorizing judges to abandon precedent and make law in accordance with their personal inclinations. Some judges and lawyers are not comfortable with a court upsetting an Act of Parliament even if it conflicts with the constitution because, according to them, such a court is being an activist. This is the common thinking that has led many apex courts to consistently rule that where a dispute may be decided without the need to invoke the constitution, this must be done. Presumably, judges should be very slow, or restrained, in nullifying laws passed by a representative body.

Interpreting the law in such a manner as to give birth to a new legal norm is very rare and is, certainly, not a daily occurrence. From the preceding discussion, it follows that while most of the work of the courts is concerned with 'the disinterested application of known law', the courts are called upon, from time to time, to decide issues that are intensely political. That duty lends itself to accusations that the decisions of the courts are political; and not legal. This much was clear in the dissenting judgment of Justice Ojwang; in the aftermath of the Kenyan Supreme Court decision in the case of Raila Odinga v Uhuru Kenyatta and Others, in 2017, in which the court annulled the presidential elections and ordered a repeat election. In his dissenting judgment, Justice Ojwang said that the decision of the majority, to order a re-run, was political; and not legal.

As indicated earlier, the rule of law would be undermined if judges were allowed to do as they pleased. The cardinal point in any discussion on judicial activism is that if it means that judges can be the law unto themselves, then that type of judicial activism is unacceptable; and even dangerous. A key aspect of judgeship is the disinterested application of the law, drawn from existing and discoverable legal sources, independently of the personal beliefs of the judge. Judicial activism should not be seen as an opportunity, by judges, to further their political preferences. That would be injurious to the rule of law and would depart, widely, from the principle of impartiality, which every judge is called upon, without exception, to adhere to as they carry out their role of adjudication.

It should never be in doubt that the rule of law applies to every human being; including those whose duty it is to apply and interpret the law. Judges are, thus, appointed to administer the law and, if necessary, to develop it; but not to undermine it. They are given substantial security of tenure in order to protect individual rights, and freedoms, from shifts in the popular will; and from the consequences of arousing the displeasure of either the public or the government. Judges must, at all times, use this power with humility and great care. I mentioned, at the start of this book, that I would reflect and draw upon on my fifteen years of experience on the bench. I must mention, at this point, that I have always endeavored, and to the best of my ability, to protect individual rights, and freedoms, from shifts in the popular will; which I have referred to above. I disclose that, in doing this, I have not only been faced with the dilemma of arousing the displeasure of some segments of society,

I have actually had first - hand experience of treading on many a toe; in the exercise of my juridical functions.

One may ask what keeps judges going; in spite of the ever present possibility that their judicial decisions could displease some people; sometimes with dire consequences. I cannot answer for others but, speaking for myself, what drives me to continue with my judicial functions, even if some of my decisions may not sit well with other branches of government or, indeed, the majority of the people at whose service I am, as a servant of the law, is the fact that it is my indefatigable duty to protect individual rights and freedoms. When I accepted the appointment to serve as a judge, first in the Labour Court and then the High Court, in my country; and, thereafter, in my present appointment in this beautiful country that is Papua New Guinea, I took an oath to protect and defend the constitution. It is this serious duty, of which I have never lost sight, that keeps me going; to this date. In addition to this, my years on the bench have taught me that judgeship is not for the faint hearted. A judge has to remain true to the constitution inspite of the challenges which that pose.

One of the most important functions of a judiciary, in a democratic state, is to shield the people from illegal conduct by government. This idea stems from the Montesquieu preposition, to which I have already alluded, that no one is above the law. This means that governments are not only obliged to respect the law, but they are under a duty to obey the law; as construed by judges. This principle can, however, only work if judges are steadfast and consistent in their application of the law. Once judicial decision-making becomes arbitrary, inconsistent, and detached from fixed, objective and fair rules of law, it will fail to command the respect, and obedience, of the people; and the system will eventually collapse. It is my personal view that the fact that judicial making has the potential to collapse a system simply shows that the judiciary is part of the governing process; in any democratic dispensation. It is an arm of government which has the responsibility to ensure that the system does not collapse because of either its judicial decisions, or the actions of the executive and the legislature. This status quo also brings out the importance of the role of the judiciary in providing the checks and balances which are needed for a democracy to remain functional. Judicial activism is one way of enabling this to happen.

It is, in particular, in the area of human rights that judicial activism, in the manner I have sought to suggest, may be very useful. South Africa, which practiced institutionalized racism for years, offers a good example of judges who literally mortgaged themselves to the philosophy of racism; that was espoused, by the Nationalist Party, for decades. When that political party came into power, in 1948, the system of apartheid was implemented; and so began what became an all embracing web of racial laws; promulgated by parliament. This resulted in discriminatory laws relating to voting rights, the rights to live in proper residential areas, freedom of movement rights; and even rights of sexual freedom.

There are many examples that demonstrate that the South African judiciary interpreted the racist statutes in such a way as to give effect to the racist policies of the ruling regime. In the case of Minister of the Interior v Lockhat, the Appellate Division, which was South Africa's highest Court of Appeal during the apartheid regime, was faced with a challenge to the validity of a proclamation which divided the city of Durban into group areas. The ground of challenge was that white people had been given the best residential areas; while only the poor areas were available to Indians. Consequently, there would be no suitable accommodation available, for some time, in the Indian areas. Mr Lockhat, an Indian, argued that the effect of the division was to discriminate to a substantial, and therefore unreasonable, degree against Indians. It was Mr. Lockhart's further argument that, in order for it to be valid, such unreasonable discrimination had to be expressly authorized by enabling legislation. The trial judge upheld the challenge on the ground that in the absence of specific authority to the contrary, in the statute, common law presumptions must prevail. The trial judge held, in effect, that the exercise of a power should be done without the inevitable result that members of different races are treated on a footing of partiality and inequality; to a substantial degree.

On appeal, this decision, which sought to avoid discrimination, was reversed by the appellate court. The effect of the appellate court's decision was that the power to discriminate was implied. That court reasoned that it was not for the court to decide whether the Group Areas Act would be for the common good of all the people. According to the appellate court, the question before the High Court was purely a legal one, namely 'whether this piece of legislation impliedly authorized, towards the attainment of its goal, the more immediate and foreseeable discriminatory results complained of'. In consequence of this decision, the Indian people were required to move out of their homes, in which they had lived for many years, and move into impoverished and undeveloped areas.

Another example in which the courts in South Africa chose to give effect to racist and repressive laws was the case of Rossouw v Sachs. The facts of the case were simple and straight forward. In 1963, a Cape Town barrister, Albie Sachs, was detained under security legislation. Sachs applied for a declaratory order that the detaining authority was not entitled to deprive him of 'any of his rights and liberties; save to detain him for interrogation and save to deprive him of access to other persons'.

Sachs sought an order, from the court, that he was 'entitled to at least the same rights and liberties, whilst in custody, as were enjoyed by prisoners awaiting trial, or other non-convicted persons who had been detained under the provisions of some other law'. Another order which Sachs sought was that he should be allowed out of his cell for reasonable and adequate exercise, and recreation, and be permitted to receive an adequate supply of reading and writing materials, subject to the scrutiny of those detaining him. Sachs, additionally, asked to be provided with the ordinary comforts of life such as soap; and similar materials.

When the case was heard, in Cape Town, two High Court judges ruled in Sachs' favour. Specifically, they found that the statute did not expressly deprive him of the right to reading and writing materials; and neither did it do so by necessary implication. The court ordered that Sachs be supplied with reading and writing materials as per his request. The police were disenchanted by that order; and appealed against it. The appeal came before the Appellate Division, which overruled the High Court's decision. The apex court pointed out that the offences covered by the statute were directed against the safety of the state, itself. It was the court's consideration that the statute impliedly authorized 'psychological compulsion'. It also recognized that the words of the statute said nothing, expressly, about whether ninety (90) day detainees had the same rights as the awaiting trial prisoners. The court sought to answer the question by determining the intention of the legislature; in enacting the detention provision. It ultimately held that the court had no duty to interpret the provision; in favour of the liberty of the subject. I believe I can confidently say that many people would agree that this judgment gave effect to racist and repressive laws, in South Africa, in the clearest of terms.

No reasonable person can dispute that, in tolerating racist and repressive laws, the South African courts fell far short, of expected standards, in carrying out their judicial duty to uphold fundamental human rights and freedoms. However, the one positive in this bleak picture was that although the overwhelming majority of apartheid judges were willing to give effect to the racist policies of the Nationalist Party, there were a few who upheld fundamental human rights and freedoms. One such judge was Justice Didcott. The fact that he was appointed to serve as a judge of the Constitutional Court, when he had served as a judge under apartheid, was a recognition that even under that abhorrent system, he sought to uphold human rights. Another judge who sought to uphold human rights, during the apartheid days, was Justice Gerald Friedman.

In most African countries, too many people whose constitutionally protected human rights have been violated have, either due to ignorance, poverty, marginalization or some other social or economic disadvantage, been unable to approach the courts for appropriate relief. Some of these structural impediments to justice can be ameliorated by judicial activism which, as I have attempted to show, is particularly critical in the defence of the constitution, and democracy, across the continent. An excellent example is the Supreme Court of Kenya's 2017 decision, ordering a re-run of the Presidential Elections. I can say, with a measure of confidence, that the decision still has the rest of sub-Saharan Africa shaken to its knees because it was one of the most consequential constitutional decisions; whose geopolitical ramifications will undoubtedly reverberate across the continent for generations yet to come.

The four Kenyan Supreme Court justices, who cast the votes to annul the President Kenyatta's election victory, were not only living up to their 'sacred' constitutional obligations to the people of Kenya, but they also showed the contemporary world, that a useful, teachable and potent lesson on genuine democracy can come from Africa; too.

Whatever criticisms are leveled against judicial activism, it cannot be disputed that it can do a great deal to ameliorate the conditions of the masses in a country. This is especially true for many African countries; in which justice remains firmly out of reach for the majority of the people. It will be noted that a lot has been said about it; but a very important aspect of judicial activism is that it has been shown to set right a number of wrongs; which have been committed by the state as well as by individuals. The majority are very often denied the protection of law due to the inefficiencies, and inadequacies, of the courts; which is also called judicial inertia or judicial tardiness. Judicial activism works to remove these occasional aberrations too.

It is worth noting that the process of removing the cited aberrations can only be furthered by honest and forthright and ethical judicial activism; and not by running down the judiciary in the eyes of the public. The greatest asset, and the strongest weapon in the armoury of any judiciary, is the confidence that it commands, and the faith it inspires in the minds of the people; in its capacity to do even-handed justice and keep the scales in balance, in any dispute.

As the discussion on judicial activism draws to a close, I wish to re-state that I have sought to argue that the term 'judicial activism' is generally misunderstood and, at times, unfairly criticized. I have also tried to show that judicial activism does not involve judges trying to routinely, and recklessly, ignore precedent; but rather, that it provides a means by which they can methodically, and systematically, try to advance the values espoused by the concept of the rule of law. In effect, I make the point that judicial activism is not a bad thing at all and that, in fact, it may be a good thing in countries with deficient democratic credentials. More significantly judges, even those that believe in judicial activism, are beholden to the universal values of justice, impartiality, truth, and integrity. They are not at liberty to do as they please. They are servants of the law and owe their fidelity to the constitution.

Judges, the world over, can take a few lessons from how judicial activism has been carefully and progressively used, in India, to enrich the rule of law. The Indian Supreme Court's willingness to tackle controversial political and legal issues, in a serious and thoughtful manner, is said to have given it prime legitimacy. It has also been said that the greatest contribution of judicial activism, in India, has been to provide a safety valve in a democracy; and a hope that justice is not beyond reach. The courts' adoption of a pro-active role, to make up for the inefficiencies of the executive, has proved beneficial to Indian society. As such, the people of India, in general, believe that if any institution or authority acts in a manner which is not permitted by the constitution, the judiciary will step in to right the wrong. This level of public confidence in an arm of government is, in my view, what every judiciary in the world should strive to attain.

Chapter Six

USE OF INTERNATIONAL AND COMPARATIVE LAW BY DOMESTIC COURTS

The issue of whether judges, in a domestic setting, should use international law is often controversial; and seen as creating an opportunity for liberal or activist judges to make law. It is largely a function of the legal system that obtains in each country, namely whether a country is a dualist or a monist state; as shall be elaborated in the course of this chapter. It is also a function of whether, in terms of the constitution of a particular country, courts are mandated to use international law, and to what extent.

In this era of globalization, judges cannot afford to remain mere spectators; believing that globalization is about goods and financial services only. Globalization also speaks to, and about, internationalization of law, where that can be done, without doing unjustified violence to domestic law. Law, especially human rights law, as enunciated in the Universal Declaration of Human Rights of 1948, needs cross fertilization in order to grow and serve the human race. This can be done without destabilizing society.

It is generally acknowledged that if the law is to be a living force, it must be dynamic and accommodating to change. It must adapt itself to fluid economic and social norms and values; and to altering views of justice. If it fails to respond to these needs, and is not based on human necessities and the experience of actual affairs of humanity, the law will one day be cast off, by the people, because it will cease to serve any useful purpose. It is, therefore, absolutely necessary that the law must be constantly on the move; and be vigilant and flexible to the current economic and social conditions of any era.

In most countries, of both common and civil law jurisdictions, there is a scope within which to use international and comparative law to interpret, and/or expand municipal, otherwise known as domestic, law. In fact, there is an increasing tendency for the courts, in many countries, to make use of international law, more particularly international human rights law, to clear ambiguities in the national laws. The use of international law, by domestic courts, is all the more important; since international human rights treaties which are ratified, although intended to be binding on states, do not, generally, involve enforceable sanctions at international level. It is, therefore, important for domestic courts to be able to use their power to impose sanctions at domestic level; in order to ensure effective respect of these rules.

The effectiveness of a constitution depends, in large measure, on its continuous cultivation and nourishment. This can best be done by extracting relevant lessons from international law and comparative foreign law; while taking care, at all times, to ensure that foreign case law, whenever it is invoked, is relevant and appropriate. Courts in Africa cannot also run away from the gradual, but progressive, internationalization of legal rules and standards in general; and constitutional law principles in particular. This means going beyond the normal common law judicial liberalism, which enables judges to refer to, cite and rely on the decisions of courts in other common law jurisdictions; as persuasive authorities.

The use of international law, especially international human rights law, as captured by leading international human rights instruments, such as the Universal Declaration of Human Rights, is justified by the fact that many modern constitutions actually derive inspiration from international law; and in particular the Universal Declaration of Human Rights, the International Covenant on Civil and Political Rights and the International Covenant on Economic and Social Cultural Rights. Because of the commonality not only in the provisions of many constitutions, but also the fact that they have been inspired by the same philosophy, it should be possible, in dealing with legal problems, to invoke these instruments; where appropriate. However, this should never be done arbitrarily, or in a manner that contradicts the clear provisions of the constitution.

It seems to me that a judicial decision has greater legitimacy, and will command more respect, if it is consistent with international law; especially an international bill of rights that is accepted, by an overwhelming number of democratic states, as representing acceptable legal norms of governing the affairs of humanity. In the midst of the transitional period of most of the new, or revised, African constitutions; and with the executive usually going out of its way to undermine judicial independence, the judiciary in Africa must ensure that its jurisprudence accords it with the highest standards of human rights, good governance and democracy. It must, also, always be remembered that the judiciary has no sword or purse. However, if its judgments fully reflect the contemporary hopes, aspirations and fears of the people, a judiciary will carry the people along; for without the people, there would be no swords and purses for any country to boast about.

International law theorists distinguish between the two types of treaty application models; namely '*monism*' and '*dualism*'. In a '*monist*' state, international treaties are included in the country's legal system and, thus, become part of the domestic law of that state. In such countries, treaties have what is known as '*self-executing status*'; and a breach of international treaty obligations may be enforceable in a court of law. An extreme example of a monist state is the Netherlands which provides, in its constitution, that certain treaties are to be directly applied. In such cases, these treaties are superior to all Dutch national laws; including the constitution of the Netherlands.

Courts, in a monist state, may directly apply treaty standards to a case before them. This is an example of the direct application of treaty obligations. If the modern monist position has a spiritual founder, it would have to be the renowned Australian legal scholar, Hans Kelsen (1881–1973), who advocated for a legal system that curbed the arbitrary exercise of power by governments. He wrote of a '*pure theory of law*'; which law is considered to be a science. Kelsen also created a legal scientific paradigm, in which the law contains its own internal basis for determining the truth; independent of other sciences. According to Kelsen, international law holds the highest authority; and national legal norms are subordinate to international norms.

Kelsen's attempt to create a system governed by universal norms has been criticized for being dominated by self-regulating lawyers. As one German jurist, Carl Schmitt opined, '*The sovereign… the engineer of the great machine (of law) has been radically pushed aside. The machine runs itself.*' In terms of the monist theory individual citizens, and not states, are the real subjects of international law.

Morgenstern argues that: "*The essence of the monist view of the relation of international law and national law is that rules of law, international and municipal law alike, are applicable to individuals, and that international law can thus be directly operative in the municipal sphere. Modern decisions have affirmed that individuals can derive rights from treaties.*"

It follows, therefore, that a specific national act of transformation of the rule, and/or rules, of international law is not required; before such a rule could be applied by a domestic court adjudicating over a dispute. It would appear, therefore, that monists have created a trans-national legal regime; that exists beyond the state.

The second type of treaty application model, namely the dualist school of thought, is premised on the preposition that law is an act of state will. The theory perceives international law and domestic law as being two distinct, and independent, legal regimes; with each having an intrinsically and structurally distinct character. It is precisely because domestic law is distinct from international law, that it is often said that a state may not rely on domestic law as a ground for repudiating an international legal obligation. The Permanent Court of International Justice explained, in the case of 'Greco-Bulgarian Communities' that: " It is a generally accepted principle of international law that, in the relations between powers who are contracting parties to a treaty, the provisions of municipal law cannot prevail over those of a treaty."

The dualist school takes the view that state law addresses the social relations between individuals; while international law regulates the social relations between states which, alone, are subject to it. Classical dualist theory argues that the source of domestic law is the will of the state itself; while the source of international law is the common will of states. Further, dualists argue that domestic and international law are differentiated by the fundamental principles to which each system is conditioned. Domestic law is conditioned by the norm that legislation is to be obeyed; whereas international law is conditioned by the rule that every agreement, duly completed, must be performed in utmost good faith.

The main difference between the types of treaty application models under discussion is that in dualist states, a treaty is not directly part of domestic law. Instead, international treaties have to be incorporated into the national law in order for their provisions to be legally binding. For a country that embraces dualism, an '*act of transformation*', by an appropriate state organ, is needed; before the provisions of a treaty can operate within the national legal system. This transformation takes various forms; such as parliamentary enactment, which directly incorporates the treaty norms into domestic law, or a statute copying all, or part of, the treaty. In dualist systems, domestic law takes precedence where there is a clear inconsistency between domestic law and international law. Perhaps the strongest argument for the dualist approach is that it preserves the sovereignty of nations; whilst accepting the importance of international law.

By way of recapitulation, it has been mentioned, above, that it is absolutely necessary that the law must be constantly on the move; and that it must be vigilant and flexible to the current economic and social conditions of any era. It has also been mentioned that the law derives momentum from many sources; among them international human rights law. Since the establishment of the United

Nations, the international community has relentlessly forged ahead; fashioning and putting in place, for the benefit of mankind, new standards and guidelines for the protection and advancement of human rights. Starting with the Universal Declaration of Human Rights, the world has seen the coming into force of numerous treaties and conventions in the area of human and peoples' rights; to which most, if not all, states have subscribed in one way or another. These international treaties and conventions have brought about change; which imposes an obligation, upon domestic courts, to protect and promote human rights; by adapting the national laws to meet the rising expectations of the peoples they serve.

The world has become one village, nay a small village, thanks to the tremendous advancement in technology; which enables peoples, the world over, to learn about changes that are taking place anywhere on the globe. The relevance of the courts, in the age of information, is buttressed by their ability to bring, to the people they serve, the changes taking place elsewhere; which positively impact on them. If the courts fail in this duty, they may well find that they are out of touch with the people's expectations and are, therefore, ill-suited to serve them. It is in this context that I reflect on how the domestic courts must deal with questions pertaining to the interpretation of international human rights norms, the techniques that they must apply, in order to strengthen those norms, and their general approach to integrating the norms into domestic law.

In some countries the basic law, i.e. national constitution, expressly provides that national courts must have regard to international law when deciding cases involving human rights and freedoms. The Republic of South Africa is one example. Section 39 of its constitution provides that, in interpreting the country's Bill of Rights, every court, tribunal or forum must promote the values, in the Bill of Rights, which underlie an open and democratic society;

based on human dignity, equality and freedom and that, in doing so *must* consider international law; and *may* consider foreign law. The courts are enjoined to do the same when developing the common law or customary law. In other countries, however, no such provision is made.

The first situation presents a domestic court with clear authority to resort to international human rights law; when confronted with a case in which municipal law does not provide an answer, or provides an anachronistic answer to the problem before it. The second situation leaves it open to the court whether or not to use international human rights law in reaching a decision. In this situation, therefore, a court has room to apply international human rights law in its decision making processes. Implicit in the court's ability, to resort to international human rights law, is the leeway it also has to use the decisions of foreign courts in reaching decisions in the domestic arena.

The common law of many countries in Southern Africa is Roman Dutch law. Botswana, Lesotho, Namibia, South Africa, Swaziland and Zimbabwe are Roman Dutch law jurisdictions. These and other countries in the same region, for example Zambia and the countries that comprise East Africa, have a common historical and political legacy; deriving from British colonial domination. This has created some legal and systemic compatibility which allows for common interpretive approaches by the domestic courts. All these countries also have dual systems of law, i.e. they have the common law operating side by side with customary law.

The courts in these countries have a duty, as spelt out, to develop both the common law and the customary law.

In emerging democracies, international human rights law is often looked upon by national governments, especially the autocratic type among them, with some degree of disfavour. They view the standards that international human rights law imposes on their governance as burdensome; and being incompatible with their peoples' culture and immediate social and economic developmental needs. More often than not, this is nothing more than an excuse for such governments' failure, and reluctance, to afford their peoples the full enjoyment of fundamental rights and freedoms. Most care only about keeping themselves in power against the interest of the people; and their hypocrisy is evident from the fact that on the international stage, they are more than willing to accede to the treaties and even ratify them; when they know, full well, that they do not intend to implement them.

The apparent resistance of governments, in Africa, to a wholesale acceptance of international law instruments, or the implementation of international instruments, is not only based on the high standards which international law imposes, but on certain practical considerations, arising from the fact that these societies have two systems of law operating side by side; and sometimes in competition with each other. There is, on the one side, the common law; which generally accords with international human rights instruments. On the other side, there is customary law; which does not. In my view, it is unrealistic to ignore the impact that customary law has on the full, and effective, application of international human rights law in most African countries. It is, I think, reasonable to suggest that in any dispute where there are opportunities to develop the common law, such must be done as a first option; before a declaration of invalidity is made.

I am of the considered view that it is necessary to closely examine the role played by customary law; in inhibiting the implementation of human rights law. The threat of discrimination, in the area of personal law, impacts quite negatively on the area of political and socio-economic rights. Thus, the treatment of persons, or groups of persons, in one area of the law influences the treatment of the same persons, or groups of persons, in another area. The laws relating to personal rights and those relating to political, social and economic rights, are inextricably interconnected. I shall illustrate this by giving an example of the old constitution of Zimbabwe.

Zimbabwe has acceded to, and is therefore a party, to many international human rights treaties; including the Convention on the Elimination of All Forms of Discrimination Against Women (CEDAW), the Universal Declaration of Human Rights, the Covenant on Political, Economic and Social Rights and the African Charter on Human and People's Rights; to name but a few. However, before the 2013 version, the old constitution of Zimbabwe, which was the fundamental law of the country then, contained clauses which, necessarily, recognized African customary law; with all its discriminatory practices. Section 89 of the old constitution of Zimbabwe recognized customary law as a part of the law of Zimbabwe; with section 23 specifically providing that a law would not be considered as making discriminatory provision; if it related to matters of adoption, marriage, divorce, burial, devolution of property on death or other matters of personal law; which were governed by customary law. Thus, Zimbabwe's old constitution exempted certain matters, to which customary law applied, from the application of the bill of rights, in its entirety and, in turn, from the full application of international treaties on the same matters.

The courts in Zimbabwe have not always been consistent on the extent of the application of the bill of rights. This has been particularly so, with regard to the question of whether it applies to certain matters, to which customary law applies, such as issues of customary inheritance and other personal law matters. In a number of decisions, the highest court in Zimbabwe was seen to lean in favour of a more generous, and expansive, interpretation of the constitution intended, it seemed, to liberate women from all forms of discrimination; and at the same time to achieve, for them, equality with men. This was illustrated in such cases as Katewe v. Muchabaiwa, Jena v. Nyemba, and Chihowa v. Mangwende which were decided in 1987. There were many other cases in which the Supreme Court of Zimbabwe extended the right to inheritance to women; consistent with international human rights instruments. In making these decisions, the Supreme Court relied on international treaties as the foundation of the equality jurisprudence.

In the course of time, however, the same court changed direction. This occurred when it was urged to respect the wording of the Zimbabwean constitution, which seemed to constitutionalize discrimination against women; when it came to matters of customary inheritance and other matters dealing with personal law. This change of direction came about in the case of Magaya v. Magaya; a judgment of the Supreme Court of Zimbabwe, delivered on 6th February, 1999. The brief facts of this case were that the deceased had died intestate; leaving two wives. Both of the marriages had been contracted under African customary law. The appellant was the daughter of the deceased; by his first marriage. The respondent, who was the deceased's son, by his second marriage, claimed heirship; after the deceased's eldest son declined to lay such claim. The heirship was initially awarded to the appellant; by a community court which was presided over by a chief; who was not familiar with international human rights law.

The respondent applied to a magistrate for a re-hearing of the matter; on the ground that persons interested in the deceased's estate had not been summoned to attend the original hearing. When the matter was re-heard, the magistrate appointed the respondent as the heir; holding that under customary law, the appellant, being female, could not be appointed as heir to her father's estate; when there was a man, of the family, who was entitled to claim the heirship. The appellant was dissatisfied with the magistrate's decision; and appealed to the Supreme Court. She argued that to deny her the heirship, of the deceased's estate, was contrary to the principle of gender equality as enshrined in various international human rights instruments; to which Zimbabwe was a party. The appellant also submitted that discrimination against women, which existed at customary law, was based on their perpetual minority status which, it was argued, had been abolished by the Legal Age of Majority Act. The appellant contended that, in any event, the court had to exercise its discretionary law-making role, to ensure that women were not excluded from being appointed heiresses at customary law; and that recent authorities, in Zimbabwe, supported this conclusion.

The appellant claimed that this was a peculiar case in which special circumstances existed; in that the respondent, as the child of the deceased's second wife, was unlikely to look after the deceased's first wife and her child (the appellant). The Supreme Court came to the conclusion that the earlier cases, upon which the appellant relied, had defined the provisions of the Legal Age of Majority Act too widely, and that the Act only gave women certain competencies; and not rights which they did not have. It pronounced the respondent as the rightful heir to the deceased's estate.

The case of Magaya illustrates the dilemma that often confronts judges, that is to say, whether they ought to interpret the constitution as a whole, or they should just focus on one particular section; which appears to specifically deal with the controversy. When the Magaya case was decided, and just like other constitutions in Africa did, section 23 of the then constitution of Zimbabwe exempted the application of the bill of rights to, amongst others, matters of customary law succession. A significant aspect of the Magaya case is that the Supreme Court, of Zimbabwe, chose to give section 23 of that country's constitution, a restrictive meaning. Needless to say, that the court's attempt to reconcile the said section 23, with the broader constitutional scheme, was not satisfactory at all. It was the court's considered view that, given the wording of section 23 of the constitution of Zimbabwe, its hands were tied. It concluded, in essence, that section 23 permitted discrimination against women on matters of customary inheritance. The court did not seek to engage with the concept of dignity; which is a core foundational value in any constitution containing a bill of rights. That, in my view, was most unfortunate indeed; given the lofty responsibility that the courts have, of protecting the fundamental human rights and freedoms of all the people that they serve; without exception. Put bluntly, the conclusion of the Zimbabwean Supreme Court, in the Magaya case, was that women were less human than men; and that they could be excluded from equal participation with men, on certain resources, simply because that was the position of customary law; which was exempted from constitutional challenge. Essentially, the court found that the discrimination of women, with regard to inheritance issues, was sanctioned by the constitution, itself, which was the supreme law of the land.

The point which I am at pains to make, here, is that while the conclusion reached by the court cannot, necessarily, be said to be wrong in law, it could be said that its conclusion was not the only possible answer to the question that the court had been called upon to determine in the Magaya case. In short, the reasoning that the court adopted was not the only path available for it to tread. I say this because the court could have held that section 23 must be read restrictively, and in conjunction with the other equality provisions of the constitution. After so finding, the court could then have gone on to hold that it was impermissible to treat women less favourably than men, because women were also human; and any departure from this most certainly offended the right to human dignity and equal protection of the law. This being said, it must be readily acknowledged that the reasoning and conclusion I am suggesting the court should have adopted may not commend itself to many judges. It is, perhaps, easier for constitutions to simply prohibit any form of unfair and irrational discrimination; and not seek to exempt any aspect of customary law from application of the bill of rights.

Some jurists have pointed out that constitutional provisions which provide for discrimination against women, for instance, will be difficult to remove. This is, firstly, because that would be a departure from the patriarchal system of social organization that is prevalent in most African countries and, secondly, because the destruction of customary law is seen, by the current political leadership, as an onslaught on the African way of life. A social system in which polygamy is permissible, and generally acceptable, is not one in which the panoply of human rights can be enjoyed by all.

In today's world, the need for the equal protection of human rights is readily recognized; and one would expect every country to prioritize the protection of human rights across the board. However, the reality of the situation, in most countries, is that while governments are all too willing and ready to sign, and even ratify, international legal instruments which prohibit all forms of discrimination against women; they fail to domesticate the said instruments. The result of this is that the constitution becomes more problematic in that, notwithstanding the ratification of international legal instruments, that promote human rights, certain sections of the constitution contradict the provisions of the ratified conventions. How, then, does one explain this dichotomy, or inconsistency, other than to speculate lack of commitment to respecting rights? This state of play is a clear indication that when governments accede to international treaties, most of them do not mean what they say; otherwise they would suitably amend the provisions of their constitutions; which entrench discrimination against women. Botswana has been independent for fifty-two years and, even though it is a party to the CEDAW, it has not seen it fit to amend section 15(4) of its constitution; which is similar to section 23 of the Zimbabwean constitution.

African jurisdictions that still exempt customary, and/ or personal, law from the application of the bill of rights must muster enough courage to amend their constitutions; and align them with international human rights instruments which African governments have ratified. The fact that a significant number of people in Africa, if not a majority in some jurisdictions, are governed by customary law, is not an excuse to maintain constitutional provisions that offend the right to equality. Constitutional reforms, in the manner suggested, would ensure that rather than have two parallel legal systems in one country, each of these countries can move to a hybrid system; fusing customary law and common law and, thereby adopting a system that is more amenable to the application of international human rights law in full.

If I am to be perfectly candid, there is little point in African governments' signing, and even ratifying, pertinent international human rights legal instruments; if these will not be applied in their national courts. Essentially, it means that the signing of these instruments is an academic exercise; and the governments are advertently neglecting to offer their peoples the added, and in some cases best possible, human rights protection; which is provided by the international human rights instruments to which the governments accede.

In Botswana, courts generally refer to foreign case law in interpreting constitutional provisions, statutory, common and customary law. Section 15(4) of the constitution of Botswana is similar to section 23 of the old constitution of Zimbabwe; which the court was called upon to interpret in the Magaya case. The difference is that the courts, in Botswana, have not followed the reasoning path adopted by the Zimbabwean Supreme Court in the case of Magaya. They, have, instead, consistently refused to interpret section 15 in a manner so as to authorize discrimination against women.

The difficulties exemplified by the case of Magaya are ever present; resulting in progress that is seemingly made at one stage being erased at a later stage. It would appear that the Court of Appeal, in Botswana, has been more consistent in applying international human rights law to resolve domestic disputes. For instance, in the well-known case of Dow v. Attorney-General, 1992 BLR 119 (C.A.), the court, relying on the jurisprudence of other countries, was able to declare that a child born to a Motswana woman, and a foreigner, was a citizen of Botswana. This was after the court struck out, as being unconstitutional, a provision of the citizenship law; which prohibited such a child from becoming a citizen of Botswana. More recently, the High Court of Botswana dealt with a case that was almost on all fours with Magaya case. Unlike in that case, the court came to the conclusion that the female child of a deceased Motswana man was entitled, contrary to the customary law of the tribe to which the deceased belonged, to be declared heiress to his estate. This was despite the fact that there was a male member of the family who, under customary law, was otherwise the heir. The case in which it was decided thus is that of Mmusi, aforementioned.

The issue in the Mmusi case, in brief, was that the court was called upon to strike down a customary law; which was to the effect that only the last male child could inherit the family homestead on the death of the parents, even where there were other siblings. The specific challenge, in the case, was raised by a female sibling; who contended that this customary rule of intestate succession violated section 3 (a) of the Botswana constitution, which guaranteed equal protection of the law to all Batswana; regardless of gender considerations, among other criteria. The court found in favour of the female sibling; and stuck down the customary practice as being in violation of the constitution.

In the Mmusi *case,* the court looked at international jurisprudence; and at how courts in other countries have dealt with similar questions. After referring to the relevant international instruments, the court referred to cases from South Africa, Ghana, Kenya and India. It came to the conclusion that the customary law that was sought to be impugned, in so far as it discriminated against women, was unconstitutional; as it offended the right to equality and equal protection of the law entrenched in the Botswana constitution. An appeal against the decision was dismissed not on constitutional grounds, but on the ground that the customary law sought to be impugned did not discriminate against women. The court, however, said that if it did, then it would be unconstitutional.

It cannot be doubted that domestic courts have a very important role of interpreting municipal law; in a way that strengthens human rights norms in their jurisdictions. The human rights regime offers great scope for the courts to protect and advance human rights. We must always be aware of the techniques, used by governments, to defeat the progressive realization of human rights. A significant expression of the growing trend to use international human rights law to influence domestic law took place in February 1988, in Bangalore, India, through the adoption of the Bangalore Principles. The meeting was chaired by Justice P. N Bagwati, the former Chief Justice of India. It, therefore, makes sense to have regard to the Bangalore principles; which set out the circumstances under which domestic courts may employ international law.

The Bangalore Principles declare that:

'There is a growing tendency for national courts to have regard to international norms for the purpose of deciding cases where the domestic law - whether constitutional, statute or common law – is uncertain or incomplete'.

'It is within the proper nature of judicial process and well-established judicial functions for national courts to have regard to international obligations which a country undertakes – whether or not they have been incorporated into domestic law – for the purpose of removing ambiguity from national constitutions, legislation or common law'.

In effect, the Bangalore Principles stated that:

1. International law is not, as such, part of domestic law in most common law countries;

2. Such law does not become part of domestic law until Parliament so enacts, or the judges declare the norms thereby established to be part of domestic law;

3. Judges will not declare such norms automatically, simply because they are part of international law or are mentioned in a treaty – even one ratified by their own country;

4. Where an issue of uncertainty arises (by a gap in the common law, obscurity in its meaning, or ambiguity in a relevant statute), a judge may seek guidance in

the general principles of international law, which are accepted by the community of nations; and

5. From this source material, a judge may ascertain, and declare, what the relevant rule of domestic law is. It is the action of the judge, incorporating the rule into domestic law, which makes it part of domestic law.

It is abundantly clear that the Bangalore Principles provide a very useful guide to making use of international law at domestic level. However, the increasing trend of courts and tribunals, all over the world, to invoke international law in order to clear ambiguities and fill gaps in national legislation is not without critics. Some of the criticism, which appears in literature, is that:

Treaties are typically negotiated by the executive arm of government; as the modern manifestation of the state. They may, or may not, reflect the will of the people.

Some commentators express skepticism about international courts, tribunals, or committees which pronounce upon international law; arguing that these structures are made up of persons whose legal regimes are different from theirs.

Some commentators have expressed concern that some of the international conventions are expressed in a language which lacks precision. This means that those who use them may be tempted to read, into their broader language, what they hope, expect or want to see.

Finally, some critics caution against undue, or premature undermining of the sovereignty of a country by judicial fiat, and against compromising the authority of every country's democratically accountable law makers; to develop domestic legislation in their own way.

At the end of the day, it is fair to say that the use of international law, by domestic courts, does not necessarily undermine the sovereignty of national law making institutions. This is because the courts acknowledge that if those institutions have made clear laws, then national laws prevail; even where these conflict with international law. To introduce a principle of international law requires a gap or ambiguity of a local law, i.e. statute or constitution; and giving effect to international law, where a country has formally ratified a relevant treaty, does no more than give substance to the act which the executive has taken.

The main conclusion that can be drawn from this chapter is that, in contemporary times, courts all over the world, including those in common law countries, have progressively invoked international law to clear ambiguities in national legislation. In some jurisdictions, the courts have used international law to develop the common law, and also to fill any gaps that may exist in legislative frameworks. These common trends, which are found in different countries and in all legal systems, are gaining momentum, as more jurists appreciate the potential of international law to inform and shape national law; and vice-versa.

The Bangalore Principles, which have been referred to above, have clearly shown that international law can be used as a source of law or tool of interpretation; and that it can at the same time be used to fill gaps, inconsistencies and ambiguities. International law can also assist lawyers' fashion their arguments in a manner that enrich local jurisprudence. An interesting fact, worth mentioning, about the Bangalore Principles is that in the early days, following their formulation in 1998, some judges and lawyers tended to regard international law as some form of heresy. Happily, this is slowly changing; and the courts in common law jurisdictions appear to be keener to use international law to clear ambiguities in national statutes. It is worth emphasizing that lawyers have an important role to play; in persuading the courts that the use of international law, in any given case, is proper and necessary. It is also important that lawyers invoke international law in their arguments and, thereby, open opportunities for the national courts to apply international human rights norms.

Chapter Seven

JUDGES AND THEIR PHILOSOPHICAL INCLINATIONS

We live in a world in which citizens are increasingly turning to the courts to resolve the controversies of the day. In their pursuit of justice, it is becoming quite common for people to ask certain questions such as: 'Who is the judge and what are his/her inclinations?' Another question that is often asked is 'does philosophy matter in the work of a judge?'

I recall, in 2015, that the President of Botswana, in addressing a judges' conference, suggested that these days, when any matter comes up for litigation in court, people ask the question 'who is the judge', in order to get a sense of how the matter may be determined. The President was, in effect, suggesting that even government officials ask the same question. It appears that it is not only the ordinary people who may think that it matters who the judge is, but even high placed politicians think the same and it is not difficult to see why. The reason is that a judge's background, and/or inclination, is not without relevance in their resolving of the controversies of the day. I have come to take the view that whether consciously or not, a judge's interpretative process is informed by some elements of well-known philosophical schools of thoughts.

The idea of '*who the presiding judge is matters* ' is the reason for the common phenomenon of judge, or forum, shopping. This is a situation in which litigants, especially lawyers, would seek to have their matter (s) determined by their preferred judge. To underscore just how real this phenomenon is, I understand that, in some jurisdictions, even Chief Justices forum shop and when called upon to constitute a panel to preside over 'sensitive national issues', they choose whichever judge they think is 'suitable' to be part of the panel. Apparently, this selection is done without the Chief Justice following any rational and objective criteria, such as seniority and qualifications. Needless to say that whichever way it is looked at, this practice is plainly wrong, as it simply makes the public lose confidence in the judicial system. I seize this opportunity to unreservedly add that any judiciary in which this undesirable practice is entertained is clearly failing in its duty to impartially protect human rights and freedoms for the benefit of the society which it serves.

As discussed in earlier chapters, any functional modern democracy requires a judiciary that is independent, impartial, courageous and prudent; in order for the rule of law to be upheld. These are attributes which every judiciary must strive to attain, and preserve, in carrying out its functions as a third arm of government.

To give an example from my own experience, when I started work in the Supreme Court of Papua New Guinea,

I was highly impressed when the Chief Justice called for volunteers to preside as a panel over a matter. To me, this clearly meant that the Chief Justice had no personal interest in the matter; and any judge could preside over it. I think it is quite obvious that this level, and spirit, of transparency inspires public confidence in a judiciary. Flowing from this, and with the greatest of respect to my judicial kin, I think many, who are clothed with similar authority, could take a leaf from the leadership style of the Chief Justice of Papua New Guinea; in order to ensure fairness in the dispensation of justice and also to defeat the practice of forum shopping. Happily, not all is lost; as there are some jurisdictions which are taking active steps to curb the issue of forum shopping. Some countries have attempted to do this by removing the human element; in terms of who should be assigned to preside over a particular case. To give an example, in Botswana, judges are assigned cases, randomly, by a machine; and not even a Chief Justice has authority to select a judge to preside over a matter. While people may hold different views over this practice, it is at least safe to say that no bias or emotion is expected from a machine in the allocation of cases.

In this chapter, I provide a snapshot of pertinent legal theories; in order to provide readers with a flavour of the various philosophical schools of thought; which may, consciously or unconsciously, inform judges in the course of interpreting the law. From the outset, I make it known that some of the philosophical theories, which I discuss, may constitute the unarticulated premise of a judgment.

A starting point, in this discussion, is that no one who is experienced with the law, and the literature on jurisprudence, would be surprised to learn that judicial philosophies matter. This is so because no judge ascends to the bench as an ideological virgin. Most judges, especially those of the positivist outlook, falsely subscribe to the notion of judicial neutrality, namely, that judges are neutral umpires; who apply the law neutrally and without regard to their philosophical outlook, sympathy and sense of humanity. This genre of judges believes in the fairy tale that judges only interpret the law and that they view 'ground breaking' judgments with disdain. Additionally, such judges contend that their duty is to stabilize the gigantic ship which is the state; and also to safeguard it against heady winds that may destabilize it. These are the executive minded justices that Lord Artkin once said he viewed with disdain.

It has become necessary for scholars to reflect on the proper nature and function of law. Analytical clarity, and jurisprudential reflections, on the nature of law and justice can enhance better understanding of the role of the courts. Legal philosophy has an important role to play in defining, and defending, the values that underpin a constitutional democracy that is based on the rule of law. To this extent, I argue that the best way to understand the functioning of a judicial mind is to factor, to the extent proportionate and reasonable, the part played by a judge's philosophy; in swinging a decision in the other direction. I stretch my argument to add that in any high stake constitutional dispute, involving an exercise of value judgment, the philosophy of a judge, and his/her views on particular constitutional issues, matter enormously.

It is a fact that a judge's belief system, his/her background, education, sense of humanity and life experiences play an important role in his/her adjudication of disputes; although this may not find expression in the clearest of terms in a judgment.

Professor Ronald Dworkins was correct in asserting, as he did, that lawsuits have a 'moral dimension' that may appeal to judges in different ways. This illuminating proposition is extremely useful in resolving a legal dispute. The 'moral dimension' of a case, that lends itself to this judicial analysis, is best explored by identifying the philosophical inclinations of a judge. In putting this into proper context, I must consider the dominant philosophical theories of law. The first of these is the natural law theories.

Proponents of natural law often assert that we cannot theorize about law, or understand society, unless we appreciate what is good, and what is not good, for society. In other words, natural law theorists assert that morality is part of law.

The Roman lawyer, Cicero, asserted that true law resonates with reason; and is in agreement with nature. He further asserted that true law was of universal application, everlasting and was promulgated by God. This is a classical assertion of the doctrine of natural law; which has been invoked to justify both revolution and reaction. For instance, during the 6th century BC, the Greeks described human laws as 'owing their importance to the power of fate; which controlled everything'. Natural law is found in Cicero's Latin explanation of the Greek Stoic philosophers; who emphasized virtue, morals and ethics as appropriate guiding principles of behaviour. Starting with Homer, the classical Greek philosophers developed their theory of natural law, in an attempt to explain the human conditions that are subject to nature's laws. According to Greek philosophers, the way things often turn out to be, or what we term as 'fate', is actually a function of nature and order in the universe.

As early as the 5th century, St Augustine posed a polemical question: "What are states without justice, but robber bands enlarged?" According to a renowned philosopher, Thomas Aquinas, natural law is about God's sense of what is good. He asserted that while an unjust law could have some legal attributes; it did not have all the definitional elements and was, therefore, not really law. Aquinas defines law as 'a rule and measure of acts, whereby man is induced to act or is restrained from acting ... the rule and measure of human acts is the reason, which is the first principle of human acts ... law is something pertaining to reason.' This was, some might say, quite a mouthful of a definition; and that may well be so. But a principal contribution of Aquinas's theory, on natural law, is its reference to reason and the common good. His theological perspective views man as a composition of body and soul; capable of sensorial perceptions. Thomas Aquinas argued that natural law was discernible by all. He was emphatic that 'the natural law is promulgated by the very fact that God instilled it into man's mind; so as to be known by him naturally.' In other words, natural law is reflective of the nature of human beings.

According to Aquinas, natural law is the idea that good must always prevail over evil. He contended that as human beings, we had a duty to conduct ourselves reasonably; and to endeavor to do the best to fellow human beings. Aquinas' conceptualization of natural law suggests, in effect, that laws which conflict with notions of reasonableness and justice lose their moral power to bind. On the basis of this reasoning, a government that abuses its authority, by enacting laws which are unjust, forfeits the right to be obeyed, because it lacks moral authority.

In England, natural law was popularized by Sir Blackstone's 'Commentaries on the Laws of England' (1723–1780); by which he asserted that English law derived its authority from natural law. This assertion was subsequently dismissed, by Jeremy Bentham, as being fanciful.

There are other theorists, such as Hobbes, John Locke and Jean-Jacques Rousseau, (1712–1778), whose views are important in understanding the concept of natural law. Hobbes contended that law and government are required, if we are to establish order and peace in society. Hobbes considered peace as the first law of nature. The second law of nature, which he asserted, was that we mutually divest ourselves of certain rights, such as the right to take another person's life, so as to achieve peace. Hobbes conceptualized life as a social contract; with agreements that should not be breached. He, however, acknowledged that since human beings tended to be selfish, they could, for instance, breach agreements not to steal; in the hope of evading detection.

John Locke theorized that the idea of social contract, as propounded by Hobbes, was intended to preserve natural rights to life, liberty, property, and the enjoyment of private rights, i.e. the pursuit of happiness. He argued that our natural right to freedom, for instance, is constrained by the law of nature; and its directive that we should not harm each other in 'life, health, liberty, or possessions'. Locke advocated a representative government, with limited authority, and characterized by checks and balances among branches of government. Such a government also had to have respect for individual liberty.

Jean-Jacques Rousseau, (1712–1778), conceptualized natural rights in a manner that was, arguably, more expansive than that of Hobbes and Locke. For instance, as far as he was concerned, as long as a government represented the 'general will' of the people, it was free to do almost anything. In this assertion, one can discern both democratic and totalitarian inclinations. Rousseau's concept of 'general will' is tied to his concept of sovereignty which, he asserted, must be exercised for the common good.

Natural law theory seemed to wane in the 19th century; with writings such as those of Hume. Dave Hume (1711–1776), in his *'Treatise of Human Nature'*, contends that moralists seek to derive an 'ought' from an 'is'. In arguing as he does above, Hume sought to suggest that facts about the world or human nature cannot be used to determine what ought, or ought not, to be done. However, the 20th century seemed to witness a renaissance of natural law theory. The Charter of the United Nations and the Universal Declaration of Human Rights of 1948 are considered, by many, as reflecting elements of natural law. The American jurist Leon Fuller, (1902–78), developed a theory that demonstrated a connection between law and morality. He contended that rules are necessary to govern human conduct; and that such rules must observe eight principles, namely generality, promulgation, non-retroactivity, clarity, non-contradiction, possibility of compliance, constancy and congruence between declared rule and official action.

John Finnis,(1940) an Oxford Legal theorist, in his treatise '*Natural Law and Natural Rights*', restated the Aquinian tenets of natural law; emphasizing that the purpose of moral beliefs was to provide an ethical structure to the pursuit, by individuals, of the basic necessities of life. Finnis contended that communal life must promote, rather than hinder, individual prosperity and happiness. In essence, Finnis contends that the overriding rationale of natural law theory is to establish what is good for human beings.

The central claims of natural law theorists, that assert the connection between law and morality, are contested by legal positivists. The term 'positivism' refers to the law as prescribed, or promulgated. The essence of legal positivism is the view that law has to be some kind of a command from a lawful authority and such law must be ascertainable or verifiable. Legal positivism rejects the theory of natural law; that law exists independently from human enactment. However, it does not follow that legal positivists are indifferent to moral questions. They contend that the law, as laid down, must be distinguished from the law as it ought morally to be. Leading positivists, such as Professor H.L.A. Hart, (1907 -1992), have argued that it is not a given that because the law has been prescribed, by a lawful authority, then it must be obeyed for that reason alone; notwithstanding that it may be unjust. Hart has also argued that the mere certification of something as legally valid is not conclusive of the question of obedience because, ultimately, any law may have to be submitted to moral scrutiny.

One of the foremost legal positivists, Jeremy Bentham, in many of his writings, dismissed natural law as nothing other than 'private opinion in disguise' or 'mere opinion of men self-constituted into legislatures'. He was not fond of unwritten law; arguing that it is intrinsically vague and uncertain, and that it cannot provide a reliable public standard; which can reasonably be expected to guide behavior.

John Austin, who is considered a student of Bentham, is generally regarded as the founder of legal positivism. Bentham was instrumental in the founding of the University College of London; and the appointment of John Austin to the Chair of Jurisprudence at the University. During his tenure as Chair, Austin published his lectures under the title '*The Province of Jurisprudence Determined*'. As a disciple of Bentham, Austin's theory of legal positivism is based on the idea of law, as a command by a sovereign authority. According to Austin, anything that is not a command is not law. This conceptualization of law as the command by sovereign authority meant, according to Austin, that customary law and public international law are not law; because they are both not traceable to any sovereign authority. Just like Aquinas did, Austin conceded that the law had moral content to it.

The theories of both Bentham and Austin are characterized by the idea of a sovereign who issues commands. For his part, Austin divided the laws that guide human behavior into three categories. The first was divine law, the second positive law and the third was positive morality. Divine law would include 'revealed law'; which was established by God. Positive law was that created by the sovereign of a community, such as a legislative body, while positive morality would include positive laws and contemporary attitudes. Austin taught that God's law was superior to positive law. As for positive law, his teaching on this type of law was that it was judged to be moral, or immoral, depending on how it served the welfare of others. Austin believed that all laws were coercive commands that must serve the general welfare.

Professor Hart, who is considered to be the father of modern legal positivism, formulated his '*The Concept of Law*', which is the most widely accepted theory of Austin's positive law. Hart considered that human beings, by their very nature, must be subject to rules because not only are they not infallible, but they tend to be selfish; and the resources that they need to share are limited. He, further, pointed out that human beings need law because they cannot be relied upon to co-operate with other human beings.

Another legal positivist, Hans Kelsen (1881–1973), propounded a rather complex theory of law; in which he asserted that the law needed to be understood as a system of 'oughts' or 'norms'. He asserted that law was hierarchical; and that at the base of any legal system was the foundation of a legal system that is superior to all other forms of law. He argued that law was no less a science, than was chemistry or physics. Kelsen advocated that law must be cleansed of impurities such as morality, sociology, psychology and political theory.

Another modern day legal positivist, Joseph Raz (1939), maintains that the moral content of law is not absolute or inherent, but is contingent upon the content of the law; and the circumstances of the society to which it applies. Raz rejects the notion that there is a general moral obligation to obey the law. He suggests, instead, that law is value neutral.

Ronald Dworkin is regarded as one of the most outstanding critics of legal positivism. He regarded the law as an interpretative process; under which individual rights are extremely important. Dworkin contests the view of many positivists that when a judge is faced with a difficult case, to which no statute or previous decision applies, then that judge exercises discretion on what seems, to him or her, to be the correct answer. According to Dworkin, a judge's duty is to interpret the law on the basis of existing legal materials; and not to make it. Dworkin's critique of legal positivism is founded on his contention that the law ought to 'take rights seriously'. According to Dworkin, individual rights must trump all other considerations. He roundly contends that rights would be seriously compromised if judges exercised discretion, and decided cases, on the basis of what seemed correct to them; as individuals.

Dworkin also, righteously, frowns upon the idea that individual rights can be subordinated to the welfare of society. In his famous book, *'The Law's Empire'*, Dworkin argues against conventionalism and pragmatism; in the adjudicatory process. He states that conventionalism and pragmatism fail to provide a strong defence to individual rights. In Dworkin's vision of 'law as integrity', a judge must not give effect to his, or her, own moral or political convictions; or even to those convictions which he, or she, thinks that the legislature, or the majority of the populace, would approve. Dworkin argues that the idea that law consists in merely following conventions may provide weak protection to rights. He insists, instead, that judges must regard precedence as part of the long story that they must consider; and then continue according to their personal judgment of how to make the developing story as good as it can be. According to Dworkin, judges must be regarded as authors engaged in a chain novel, with each one of them being required to craft their individual piece; which the next judge, writing their own piece, must connect to. Each novelist must seek to make the story coherent and logical. Dworkin criticizes pragmatism because, in his view, it rests on a claim that judges do, and should, make whatever decisions seem, to them, to be best for the community's future.

In his critique of legal positivism, Dworkin also maintained that a stronger defence of rights benefited society because it provided predictability and fairness; by securing equality amongst citizens. He believed that, in providing predictability, the law provided safeguards against partiality, deceit and corruption. The thesis by Dworkin, on his taking rights seriously, is informed by the liberal view that 'government must treat people as equals'; and that it (government) may not impose any disadvantage, or constraint, on any citizen; which that person could not accept without abandoning a sense of equal worth. Dworkin subscribes to a view of political morality which is informed by three considerations, namely justice, fairness and procedural due process.

On the other hand, Philosophers, called Utilitarians, take a slightly different angle on law and its purpose. They argue that nature has placed humankind under the governance of two masters, namely pain and pleasure, and that, essentially, human life is about achieving pleasure and avoiding pain. The notion of utilitarianism relies on case precedent; but allows for judicial review authorizing the overruling of a law that is no longer effective. It is connected to tradition and is less concerned with subjective personal judgments. A defining feature of utilitarianism is the ability of law to engender happiness and in that regard, utilitarianism emphasizes on the achievement of happiness for the greatest number of people.

According to Utilitarians such as John Stuart Mill, who was one of the most influential philosophers in England during the nineteenth century, justice lies in the maximization of happiness. Mill was a protégé of his father, James Mill, who was a proponent of the theories of Jeremy Bentham, the founder of utilitarianism, and John Austin, the founder of legal positivism; both of whom were Utilitarian philosophers. In my considered view, Mill was properly characterized as an empiricist; in that he would only accept and believe a proposition if it could be experienced. One could trace the logic of the American legal realism movement to Mill's theory of utilitarianism. In his publication titled '*Taking Rights Seriously*', Ronald Dworkin states that Mill "deploys a pessimistic theory of human nature, emphasizes the value of cultural and historical constraints, on egotism, and insists on the role of the state in educating its citizens away from individual appetites and toward social conscience".

There is another group of philosophers called 'legal realists'. Justice Holmes is considered to be one of the leading exponents of American realism. In his work titled '*The Path of the Law*', *he* expressed strong disagreement with those who argue that law is something different from what is decided by the courts. Justice Holmes stated that "the prophecies of what the courts will do in fact, and nothing more pretentious, are what I mean by the law". Although legal realism may be difficult to define, a close definition is that it is 'a method of analyzing a transaction, and allowing the facts to dictate their own rules, rather than imposing external regulations'. Legal realists tend to be multi-disciplinary in approach. In their reasoning, they tend to place reliance on history, economics and sociology.

Drawing from the theory of legal realism, it is my view that as society evolves, and more cases of a complex nature reach the courts, it should be possible to modify the rules of law and integrate science into adjudication, particularly on human rights issues. For instance, on matters of public health, it is imperative that judges must allow evidence and science to inform their conclusions.

In the circle of philosophers, there is a multi-disciplinary band; which is often lumped together as belonging to the Critical Legal Studies (CLS) school of thought. CLS emerged in the 1970's in the United States; essentially as a left critique of orthodox legal doctrine. It employed a multi-disciplinary approach, drawing on sociology, politics and philosophy, among other disciplines, to critique the law. Critical Legal Studies scholars do not think that there is a fundamental difference between law and politics. They deny the neutrality of law, pointing out that it (law) is a coercive system of rules that serve the interests of the dominant sections of society. CLS often applies Marxist ideas, one of which is that law cannot be neutral. Another attribute of CLS is that it rejects the notion that law can be a panacea of all societal ills. The Brazilian theorist, Robert Unger (1947) is considered to be one of the foremost proponents of CLS. He refutes the orthodox legal theory which asserts that law can be deployed to answer every conceivable problem.

From the various examples that have been cited, above, it can be seen that each era has had its share of philosophers. In addition to those referred to, there is yet another group of philosophers which puts humanity at the center of decision making. One such philosopher was Immanuel Kant. He emphasized the importance of the element of 'humanity' in taking decisions. This philosopher contended that anyone who made a decision had to have regard for the dignity of all the persons involved in the dispute. This, essentially, meant that an individual was to always be treated with respect; and not as an object to be manipulated as a means to accomplish an ulterior motive. Kant's thoughts on major philosophical questions are encapsulated in three of his major works: '*Critique of Pure Reason*,' *Critique of Practical Reason*', and '*Critique of Judgment*'. His moral philosophy required that due attention be paid to the nature of relationships and the legal obligations engendered thereby.

Other philosophers such as John Rawls were concerned with issues of the liberty of an individual being secured by law. In his writings, John Rawls asserts that a legal system is a coercive order of public rules which is addressed to rational persons; for the purpose of regulating their conduct and providing the framework for social cooperation.

According to Rawls, when these rules are just, they establish a basis for legitimate expectations. This is so because these rules would then constitute grounds upon which persons can rely on one another; and rightly object when their expectations are breached. Rawls strongly believed that the liberty of an individual should be compatible with the fair distribution of economic opportunities; which caters for the interests of the least advantaged.

At the end of the day, the extent to which a judge subscribes to one of the philosophical schools that have been, briefly, discussed above, or a combination of a broad spectrum of theories, may be an indicator as to whether he or she is regarded as a conservative or liberal judge. Conservative judges tend to take a strict, constructionist, approach to constitutional interpretation. In literature, this strand is also called 'judicial restraint'; and the type of restraint may either be loose or strict. Judges who believe in judicial restraint frown upon the idea of judges making law. Conservative judges often insist that the courts should interpret the constitution in accordance with the intention of the framers; and where rights, or benefits are not expressly conferred, such judges tend to be reluctant to infer them from the broader scheme of the constitution.

There are several elements of conservatism. These include a willingness to limit individual rights where they conflict with government authority; preference and respect for private property; deference to governmental decisions and reluctance to upset same; and concern for law and order, often over liberty and equality. Other elements of conservatism are having less enthusiasm to embrace international law; deciding cases on the narrowest of possible grounds, including the avoidance of constitutional decisions when possible; respect for precedent and concern that constitutional decisions be grounded on literal textual provisions. Yet other elements include reluctance, or even avoiding, to answer political questions that may require legal resolution; adherence to restrictive rules of standing and often insisting that litigants must have standing to sue where their rights, and not necessarily interests, have been, or are about to be, violated, and lastly, but not the least, reluctance to provide, or issue, advisory opinions. Justice Scalia of the US Supreme court, who passed on in 2016, is often cited as an example of a conservative judge who met a number of the above cited attributes.

When they are interpreting the constitution, conservative judges are particular about giving effect to the intention of its framers. This judicial philosophy is called 'originalism'. It is an interpretation method that seeks to hold the constitution hostage, to those departed, but has no traction with modern constitutional lawyers. It is worth noting that originalism runs counter to the view held by many liberals; that a constitution must be interpreted as a living document. Conservative judges believe that an expansive, and generous, interpretation of the constitution allows judges the opportunity to legislate and often to be the overlords of the constitution. They take the view that to regard the constitution as a living document allow courts to facilitate change; which is not their duty. Conservative judges detest judicial activism with a passion; believing in the fairy tale that judges do not make law, when in actual fact judges are the best lawmakers. Judges who are conservative tend to believe that the principles derived from previous decisions form a body of controlling law; for future decisions. They condemn liberals for striving for 'justice' in a case, based on their own philosophies and socio-economic values and, in the process, according settled legal principles little or no weight. According to conservative judges, judicial power should never be exercised for the purposes of giving effect to the will of the judge, but rather that of the legislature, which is the primary lawmaker.

Inspite of their firmly held belief in originalism, conservative judges occasionally veer to the left. For instance, Justice Scalia surprised many members of the legal fraternity, when he voted to uphold free speech in the Texas flag burning case. The judge acknowledged the discomfort in seeing the flag burnt; but could not fathom those who wanted to punish the flag burners. He recognized that the ability to speak one's mind, and to challenge authority without fear of recrimination by the State, was the essential distinction between life in a free country and that in a dictatorship. Justice Scalia understood that although the flag was a fundamental symbol of American nationhood, a proper constitutional reasoning required the courts to make decisions which they did not necessarily like, but which had to be taken because they were right. It was the judge's view that, to that extent, it was imperative that the flag protect those who held it in contempt.

Justice Scalia weighed in his conservative views in the case of Bush v Gore; and literally helped hand over the 2000 election victory to President George W. Bush. Many constitutional scholars have criticized the decision as being wrong. In the dissenting judgment of Justice Stevens, with whom Justice Ginsburg and Justice Breyer agreed, the majority decision, in essence, discredited the independence and impartiality of the judiciary. Justice Stevens concluded that: "*Time will one day heal the wound to that confidence that will be inflicted by today's decision. One thing, however, is certain. Although we may never know with complete certainty the identity of the winner of this year's presidential election, the identity of the loser is perfectly clear. It is the nation's confidence in the judge as an impartial guardian of the rule of law.*"

In June 2015, when the Supreme Court upheld the Obama Care, Justice Scalia, was scathing against the majority decision; which allowed the federal government to provide nationwide tax subsidies to help Americans to buy health insurance. He accused the majority of twisting the meaning of plain words saying, in the course of his dissent, that: "*the court's decision reflects the philosophy that judges should endure whatever interpretive distortions it takes in order to correct supposed flaw in statutory machinery. That philosophy ignores the American people's decision to give Congress all legislative powers enumerated in the Constitution.*"

Justice Scalia was equally scathing, in his dissent, in the 2015 landmark case in which the Supreme Court upheld the right to same sex marriage; by a majority of one. He came hard on the majority decision, writing that the ruling was 'at odds not only with the Constitution, but with the principles upon which our nation was built'.

Justice Scalia's views reflect the approach of conservatives; with respect to the task of judging. The tragedy of conservative/liberal contestation, over what the task of judging entails, is often characterized by self-serving criticism, with the right accusing the left of judicial activism; which, as has been explained, is concerned with shaping the law in accordance with a judge's socio-economic views or philosophy. However, history would testify that conservative elements, just like liberals, may occasion violence to plain words; in order to give effect to their world outlook.

Liberals, on the other hand, do not consider legal interpretation to be a mechanical enterprise. Liberal judges tend to be open-minded; and may be influenced by societal, or political, changes. They accept the view that in the course of interpretation, or in the course of applying the law to unique circumstances, they may make law. Liberal judges are often called activist judges. Without revisiting the meaning of the term judicial activism, it has been explained, in the earlier chapters of this book, that quite often, judicial activism is misunderstood, or distorted, to mean that judges interpret the law in a manner that accords with their personal or political preferences. Judicial activism involves judges bringing to bear, on a particular statutory or constitutional interpretation, a meaning that accords with the dictates of an evolving society and its aspirations and, where appropriate, judges developing the law. Ultimately, however, no judge, whether conservative or liberal, is permitted to twist the law to accord with his or her personal preferences.

Liberal Judges consider that the ultimate objective of the law should be the welfare of society. Perhaps the most significant advance, in the modern science of law, is the change from the analytical to the functional attitude. In the enterprise of judging, justice must be the overarching objective that directs the reasoning process of judges. It is necessary to mention that history has recorded that most of the expansive rights of accused persons, pursuant to notions of fair trial, such as the right of an accused to be afforded adequate facilities for his defence which may include, in some jurisdictions, the right to access the investigating diary of police officers, is on account of liberal judges.

It is fair to say, as some kind of crude generalization, that liberals tend to be pro-defence in criminal procedure cases, pro-minorities in civil rights cases, pro-individual against government, in cases involving free speech and liberty, and pro-liability in individual injury cases. Let me hasten to add that by the use of the word 'pro', it is not being suggested that liberal judges will decide a case without due regard to the facts and the law. What it means is that where there is ambiguity, in the course of interpreting a statutory or constitutional provision, such judges are more likely to interpret it in a way that vindicates, rather than erodes, rights.

Liberal judges tend to believe that courts should read the constitution expansively; and should not limit themselves to what is explicitly stated. They believe that a constitution must grow and adapt to new circumstances. In the United States of America, and other western democracies, scholarly research has established that Supreme Court justices' jurisprudential philosophies, values and policy preferences have a bearing on their decisions. Researchers, in the US, have carefully analyzed the judgments of the Supreme Court justices, as well as their upbringing, the political climate under which they were appointed and their ideological preferences; in order to determine how they are likely to vote in any controversial case of national importance. Using the statistical analysis of

Supreme Court votes, scholars found a positive co-relation between their ideological preferences and their verdicts. Quite significantly, and using very sophisticated statistical analysis, researchers have also found that the policy preferences of many justices tend to shift over time.

It is generally fair to say, at least in terms of the preponderance of literature, that liberals are more supportive of the exercise of civil liberties and the rights of persons that stand accused of committing crimes. They are similarly supportive of the expansion of rights and democratic space; and measures aimed at improving the lot of the poor, as opposed to the rich. Liberals tend to throw their weight behind calls for minimum wages; and a wide array of union rights; such as freedom of association, the right to collective bargaining and the right to picket and strike.

Other than the broad classification of conservative and liberal judges, there is often a third category, termed moderate judges. What, then, are the defining characteristics of moderate judges? Judicial moderate philosophy is not as easy to define as judicial conservatism or liberalism. It can be said to be a philosophical position that is in between conservative and liberal perspectives. One characteristic of moderate judges is that they share a lot in common with conservative judges. It is of note that although moderate judges often vacillate between conservative and liberal inclinations, and tend to provide a swing vote in a panel that is evenly divided between the conservative and the liberals, moderate they are, on the main, conservative; and have strong respect for precedent. Moderate judges are also generally reluctant to deliver groundbreaking decisions. Instead, they tend to be open to persuasion to determine the case on the facts and law and not ideological considerations.

In sum, this chapter sought to provide an overview of various judicial philosophies that judges may, consciously or unconsciously, bring to bear on the adjudicative process. The extent to which judges embrace any of the various philosophical schools of thoughts may earn them the label conservative, liberal or moderate. There is nothing magical about these labels; and the boundaries that separate these classifications may not be water tight. In fact, it is fair to say that most judges go about their work without even thinking about where they fall in terms of philosophical school of thought. In the greatest number of cases, it may well be true that a judge's philosophy plays no part in their reasoning process during the course of adjudication. However, in some cases, it clearly does; irrespective of whether the judge feels that way or not.

In the contemporary world, members of the public often speculate on how judges may determine major controversies before them. This chapter has endeavoured to show that this speculation may be informed by the individual judges' backgrounds and/or judicial philosophy or, indeed, their alleged loyalties. The debate about the relationship between law and morality remains with contemporary society; as it has always done for centuries. Questions such as 'can the law be separated from morality, or can it be neutral' remain with us to this day; and are even more pertinent in cases involving the rights of lesbian, gay, bisexual and transgender people.

Chapter Eight

JUDICIAL POLITICS

I wish to begin this chapter by making the statement that to associate judges with politics is simply courting trouble. Once, at a Southern African Development Community (SADC) lawyers' conference held in Gaborone in 2017, I provocatively asked a former justice of the Constitutional Court of South Africa, Justice Zak Yacoob, whether he thought that constitutional law was just politics by another name. I do not recall, exactly, what he said; but he seemed to accept that there could be some merit in that proposition. Although my question, to my judicial brother, was intended to be intellectually provocative, the truth is that we live in a time where the power of the judiciary has driven politicians into panic mode; and a time when the judiciary is asserting its authority, more and more, as the custodian of the rule of law. The result of this is that the judiciary is, increasingly, being accused of overreaching; and failing to keep out of the political arena. In short, the judiciary is being seen as veering out of its lane; and encroaching upon the executive and the legislature.

It may be recalled that some years back, in South Africa, a newspaper called 'The Sowetan' carried a story;

in which the then Secretary General of the ANC, Gwede Mantashe, was reported as having said that the judiciary, in South Africa, was aiding in consolidating opposition to government; and that there was a great deal of hostility against government; that came from the courts. Subsequent to his remarks, his colleague in the ANC, Advocate Ngoako Ramathodi, who was the Chairperson of the Parliamentary Portfolio Committee on Justice, and also a member of the Judicial Service Commission, was reported as having, effectively, accused the courts of taking away power from the executive and the legislature and, thereby, rendering the electoral victory of the ANC useless. Suffice it to say that all these sentiments are consistent with the refrain one often hears from some ANC members, in South Africa, that they are not co-governing the country with the courts or the Democratic Alliance; which is the main opposition party in South Africa.

A few years later, still in South Africa, things seemed to take a turn for the worse; when the president's reshuffle of his cabinet was questioned in a court of law. As one can imagine, this did not sit well with some. However, the spectacle of the South African judges entertaining an application challenging a cabinet reshuffle, by a president, when this is traditionally considered to be a political matter, that judges should not entertain, is one of the visible aspects of the increasing assertiveness of the courts to get involved in issues involving the rule of law without fear or favour. Another example, yet again involving the South African courts, was the subsequent litigation on the question of whether a motion of no confidence, against a sitting president, was liable to be subjected to secret ballot; when the constitution was silent on same. All these developments have led to charges that the judiciary is being politicized.

Going by the examples which I have given, and many others which have not been mentioned, it seems to me that, quite often, there is a disconnect in appreciating the proper constitutional relationship between the executive and the judiciary. I find this to be particularly so when it comes to the constitutional obligation of the courts to respect all acts of the executive, within its lawful province, and for the executive to understand, and appreciate, that it is bound by the decisions of the courts; as to what it (executive) can lawfully do, or not do.

In consequence of these developments, some presidents are simply packing the courts with their preferred candidates; hoping that by so doing, those judges will tow their line and decide matters in accordance with the policy positions of their political parties. An example that comes to mind is President Trump, of the United States of America, who is outspoken and who, on ascending to the presidency, made it clear that he would appoint judges who would reverse the signature health policy of former President Obama; which is known as Obamacare. He also made it known that he wanted judges who would reverse the same sex marriage ruling of the Supreme Court. In essence, President Trump wants a court that will pursue the conservative values of the Republican Party.

In Africa, the phenomenon of cadre judgeship is fast gaining traction and, it has to be added, is set to politicize the judiciary and render it an extension of the executive; or the ruling parties. The question may be asked as to why I make this observation. The answer lies in the fact that in many jurisdictions, in Southern Africa, the bodies that recommend the appointment of Judges, that is to say the Judicial Service Commissions (JSC's), are dominated by members of the executive; possibly to ensure that the preferences of the executive get approved. It can hardly be contested that where the JSC's are dominated by the executive, the public tends to doubt the independence of the judiciary; especially when dealing with political questions that are of national significance.

The phenomenon of cadre judgeship has brought about very negative consequences in that, increasingly, those judges who are not embellished in it and are, instead, delivering judgments meant to protect the constitutional rights of individuals, especially the marginalized and vulnerable sections of the community, are targeted for overt and/or covert harassment. Judges who stand up for the morality of the constitution have come under heavy attack, from politicians, in an effort to frustrate them out of the judiciary. In some judiciaries, judges who have shown commitment to the rule of law have been labeled 'counter revolutionary'.

In South Africa, in response to the increasing willingness of the courts to review the actions and decisions of executive or legislative authority, some sections of the ANC have called upon parliament to pass laws that will effectively clip the wings of the courts. Increasingly, candidates for judgeship are subjected to questions intended to find out how they are likely to decide certain controversial questions; pertaining to exercise of public power by the executive and the legislature. These questions are usually disguised as routine ones; and instead of being asked, out-rightly, about how they would decide certain cases, judges are asked about their 'judicial philosophies'. Through this stratagem, politicians, in particular, hope to have an idea of how a judge is likely to decide some controversial constitutional questions.

There is growing concern, by many politicians and some scholars, that the courts are increasingly getting involved in managing public institutions and the industrial/employment relations sector (especially appointments to top state positions such as Director of Public Prosecutions and other similar positions); and that this involvement trespasses into the lane of the executive. The fact that the courts frequently intervene in policy making processes means that legislative activity must anticipate possible court challenge and, if considered necessary, seek to minimize successful challenge.

The transformation of political questions, into legal ones, is now an inevitable feature of the times that we live in; and which, in my view, can only keep on growing. The phenomenon in which the courts are, increasingly, determining political questions, which traditionally had been thought to be the preserve of either the executive or the legislature, is often called the 'judicialization of politics'. At the most abstract level, the term refers to the spread of legal rules, and procedures, into the political sphere and policy-making fora and processes. Matters that, traditionally, were thought to be highly polycentric are now entertained by the courts; and often the justification for doing so is that the constitution mandates the intervention. More often than not, where the courts are convinced that the constitution has been contravened, they deal with the matter and issue an appropriate order. Suffice it to say that this intervention does not always please certain segments of society.

The judicialization of politics, as defined above, seems to reflect the common translation of fundamental justice, into what is predominantly procedural fairness. Some authorities have argued that judicialization of this type is inextricable from the law's capture of social relationships and popular culture; and its expropriation of social conflicts. Judicialization of politics, in the modern world, is manifesting itself in several ways. Increasingly, government departments are heavily involved in issues, and programmes, concerning the welfare of the people and, in the course of doing this, they make certain decisions. Individuals who are aggrieved by the decisions of administrative authorities are approaching the courts to review, correct or set aside the offensive decision. On occasion, the courts are asked to substitute their own decisions for those of administrative authorities; and they do so; if that is the correct position to take.

The growth of administrative agencies, in the modern welfare state, has expanded the scope of administrative review by courts. More often than not, such judicial involvement, in public policy-making, is confined to procedural aspects; focusing on process, rather than substance. Judicial review of administrative action, or executive action, has become pervasive and is particularly noticeable in high policy areas such as immigration, employment and public tenders. But it is also clearly evident in countless other areas, including urban planning, public health and consumer protection.

In the United Kingdom (UK), in 1995, the court struck down a multi-million Pounds subvention to Malaysia; which was supposed to be utilized for the construction of a dam, but was tied to kickback orders for the British arms industry, and had been roundly condemned by government advisers; as a waste of money. The ground upon which the court struck down the subvention funds was that they were not authorized by the statute; pursuant to which the Foreign Secretary had purportedly acted. In a surprising move, and in order to subvert the order of the court, the British Government used different funds for the same purpose. Whilst the minister and the government obviously regarded the court as having overstepped its boundaries, or overreached into the political arena, it seems quite plain that the only thing that the court did was to test the legality of executive action, against the relevant statutory power.

An even more interesting example, of court intervention in executive action, was a split decision of the Court of Appeal in the UK, in 1996, concerning benefits of asylum seekers. The Court struck down social security regulations; which took all benefits away from asylum seekers who had not claimed asylum on entry into the UK. The Court of

Appeal held that the exclusion of impoverished foreigners, from receiving the benefits, was contrary to the law of humanity; which was inherent to all positive laws and, as such, obliged the British Government to afford asylum seekers relief; in order to save them from suffering.

Examples of the so called judicialization of politics, or the courts determining political questions, abound. As far back as 1995, the Russian Constitutional Court, in the Chechnya Case, assumed jurisdiction in a case involving a number of opposition members of the Duma, which is a legislative body in the ruling assembly of Russia, who challenged the constitutionality of three presidential decrees ordering the Russian military invasion of Chechnya. In rejecting Chechnya's claim to independence, and upholding the constitutionality of President Boris Yeltsin's decrees as lawful, the court stated that maintaining the territorial integrity, and unity, of Russia was an unshakable rule; that excluded the possibility of an armed secession in any federation.

In 2004, the Supreme Court of Israel ruled on the constitutionality, and compatibility with international law, of the West Bank barrier, which is a controversial network of fences and walls separating Israel from Palestinian territory.

Another example of courts scrutinizing a subject matter which was traditionally thought to be the prerogative of the executive, as it concerned a national fiscal and welfare policy, is illustrated by the 1995 Austerity Package Decisions (the so-called 'Bokros cases') determined by the Hungarian Constitutional Court. In that case, the court struck down the country's comprehensive economic emergency plan, which the government had introduced; the major thrust of which was a substantial cut in the government's expenditure on welfare benefits, pension allowances, education, and health care; in order to reduce Hungary's enormous budget deficit and foreign debt.

South Africa is another country in which the court exerted its authority in a matter that was considered to be the preserve of the executive. The was on account that immediately following the finalization of the constitutional negotiations, the Constitutional Court, to the surprise of many observers, asserted its authority and refused to accept a national constitutional text that was drafted by a representative constitution making body.

In 2004, the Constitutional Court of South Korea dismissed the impeachment of President Roh Moo-hyun; by South Korea's National Assembly. This case was, perhaps, the first in the history of modern constitutionalism; whereby a president, who was impeached by a legislative body, was reinstated by a judicial body.

Another example that is a manifestation of the judiciary's determination to ignore the traditional boundaries, of what courts may or may not do, is illustrated by the restoration of the 1997 Fijian Constitution, by the Fijian Court of Appeals, in the case of Fiji v. Prasad. This was another first in the history of modern constitutionalism.

In many parts of the world, the courts are increasingly being called upon to decide on matters such as party funding, campaign financing and broadcast advertising during election campaigns, the re-drawing of electoral districts and the approval or disqualification of political parties and candidates. Constitutional courts in many countries have become sites of political contestation as these courts are compelled to deal with political questions which are dressed up as constitutional issues. Recently, in South Africa, the courts were called upon to order that the National Assembly undertake a secret ballot to determine a motion of no confidence; which the opposition brought against President Zuma.

In some countries, the courts have been called upon to determine the political future of prominent leaders; through impeachment or disqualification trials. For instance, the courts approved or, indeed disapproved, the extension of the presidential terms, in office, of Colombia's President Alvaro Uribe, Uganda's President Yoweri Museveni and Russia's President Boris Yeltsin. Other politicians who have had their fate determined by the courts include Pakistan's former Prime Ministers, Benazir Bhutto and Nawaz Sharif, and the Philippines' President Joseph Estrada. One could add, to the above, corruption indictments against Heads of State; such as Italy's Silvio Berlusconi, Peru's Alberto Fujimori, Thailand's Thaksin Shinawatra and South Africa's Jacob Zuma. The courts have also dealt with 'political trials'; in which prominent opposition candidates and leaders have been disqualified or otherwise removed, from the political race, by the judiciary. As can be expected, this has attracted a chorus of objections, from some, that the courts have overreached.

The judicialization of politics is also gaining prominence in the area of elections and electoral processes. Increasingly, the courts are called upon to validate, or invalidate, the election of presidential candidates. Quite often, the losing party or candidate alleges breaches of the law in the election; and even outright rigging. In such situations, the courts have intervened, in order to determine who has been duly elected president and in the process of doing so have, unfortunately, opened themselves to unproved, and improvable, charges of partisanship. Examples in which the courts have been confronted by such charges are in the United States, in 2000, in Mexico (2006) and Kenya in 2013.

Perhaps there is no case that illustrates the politicization of the law, or the judicialization of politics, better than the 2000 election case between George W. Bush and Al Gore; in the United States of America. Many law professors, media commentators and other ordinary observers considered the intervention of the US Supreme Court, and ultimately the handing of victory to Bush, as a political act by that court. Many legal commentators argued that the decision violated the separation of powers; and that the Supreme Court should not have intervened in the matter.

For those who may not recall the events, the 2000 US elections did not produce a clear winner; on account of controversy surrounding voting re-counts in the State of Florida. The re-counts were started and stopped; as the Republicans and the Democrats could not agree on the standards to be applied. When it became clear that the stakes were far too high, and that the contest was a close call, the contestants resorted to lawsuits; in an effort to swing the ballot in their favour and send their candidate to the White House. These suits proceeded simultaneously in the State Court and Federal Court System. At its heart, the Bush and Gore case concerned the matter of the manner of vote counting, and re-counting, in the state of Florida. There were damning allegations, by the contestants, of intimidation and ballot rigging.

Ultimately, the 2000 US Presidential Election Petition was decided by a majority of one; by a court that many accused of being more aligned to the Republicans, in terms of political orientation. The split of 5–4 suggested, to many, that the decision was a political and not just a judicial one. Needless to say, the Bush camp was extremely excited, by the outcome of the case, whereas Al Gore's supporters were incensed; believing that the court was simply political.

In Mexico, a series of election appeals, and counter-appeals, culminated in Mexico's Federal Electoral Court's dismissal of leftist runner-up Andres Manuel Lopez Obrador's claim of massive fraud; by the right-wing candidate, and election winner, Felipe Calderon, in the July 2006 Presidential Election in that country. Calderon won the election by a less than 0.6 percent margin. From these examples, it can be seen that Constitutional Courts have also played key roles in deciding election outcomes in states and provinces; the world over.

Similarly, in Kenya, in the case of Raila Odinga and 5 Others v Independent and Electoral Boundaries

Commission and 3 Others, (2013), some commentators criticized the Supreme Court, of that country, for deciding the case on the basis of narrow legalism and resorting to technicalities of the rules of evidence, practice and procedure; to simply frustrate the will of the Kenyan people. The court was accused of imposing stringent standards, on the petitioners, making it virtually impossible for them to succeed. The petition, which was presented before the court by the then Leader of the Opposition, Raila Odinga, to declare the elections invalid was unsuccessful.

The extent to which the courts can enforce constitutional rights is, in large part, a function of how comprehensive a particular constitutional framework is in upholding human rights; and the commitment and professional capacity of the courts to properly interpret the constitution. Some constitutions, such as that of Botswana, entrench only civil and political rights. In some countries, such as South Africa, Malawi and Kenya, the socio- economic rights of people are also recognized, although the exact formulation differs from country to country. It follows, therefore, that the courts of Botswana, unlike their counter parts in South Africa, Malawi and Kenya, are constrained in fully enforcing socio-economic rights.

The examples that have been given above, of how the courts have been called upon to determine political matters, show that the existence of an enabling constitutional framework is critical in enforcing rights. It has also been demonstrated that a constitution which is comprehensive, and does not leave matters to the imagination or interpretation of an individual judge, is better than a constitutional framework that is sketchy and requires judges to fill in gaps, and iron out ambiguities, which may be occasioned by inadequate coverage of human rights. The importance of having a comprehensive constitution, which is devoid of ambiguity, cannot be over emphasized; because a sketchy constitutional framework opens judges up to unjustified accusations of overreaching, when they interpret constitutional provisions to expand the enjoyment of rights. For instance, a judge who interprets the right to life broadly, to include the right to water or medical treatment, may be accused of legislating; in a country where socio-economic rights are not entrenched. This is notwithstanding the fact that such an interpretation is jurisprudentially sound and defensible. Given the, sometimes misplaced, perception that the courts tend to wield too much power, to the extent of overreaching, it is safe to say that this particular line of interpretation may even breed tension between the executive and the judiciary.

In some jurisdictions, such as South Africa and Kenya, the judges are constitutionally mandated to develop transformative jurisprudence. In other words, when it comes to interpreting the constitution, the judges in these two countries are enjoined to be judicial activists. The existence of a constitutional framework that facilitates judicial activism may provide political actors, who are unable, or unwilling, to advance their policy preferences through majoritarian decision-making arenas, with an alternative institutional channel, namely the courts, for accomplishing their policy goals. This is the reason why most politicians, in South Africa, are wont of saying that the opposition political parties are trying, through constant litigation, to get from the courts that which they failed to get from the electoral process. As was noted earlier on, other critical political commentators have gone so far as to say that they were not elected to co-govern with the courts and the opposition.

The advantage of constitutions such as those of South Africa and Kenya, which mandate the courts to be transformative, in their jurisprudence, is that such constitutions also allow for what may be referred to as 'judicialization from below'. This means legal mobilization by groups and movements; that aim to advance social change through constitutional rights litigation. Therefore, in countries where Bills of Rights and active judicial review procedures have been adopted, one may expect a significant growth in the frequency, and scope, of the exercise of judicial review; and a corresponding intrusion by the judiciary into the prerogatives of legislatures and executives.

Judicial activism may even be more pronounced in countries like Kenya where, in terms of the constitution, the general principles of public international law are part of that country's laws. To this extent, the adoption of multilateral treaties, and international agreements, which contain justiciable provisions, and the accompanying establishment of adjudication, or arbitration tribunals, at the supranational level, are pre-conditions for the judicialization of international trade disputes.

The models of judicial review, which are employed by constitutional democracies, differ from one jurisdiction to the other; in terms of their procedural characteristics. This fact has important implications for the scope, and nature, of judicial review in the various jurisdictions. In some countries, abstract review, in anticipation of a dispute, is admissible. In others, it is possible to stop a bill in its tracks; if it is anticipated that the resulting law may offend the constitution. An important factor worth noting is that in most common law jurisdictions, a declaration of unconstitutionality cannot be made in the absence of an actual case or controversy.

There are some countries in which judicial review may be brought prior to a bill becoming law; or after a law, which allegedly offends the constitution, has been enacted. In Canada, for instance, judicial review is not limited to that which takes place within the context of concrete adversary litigation. The reference procedure allows both the federal and provincial governments, in Canada, to refer proposed statutes, or even questions concerning hypothetical legal situations, to the Supreme Court, or the Provincial Courts of Appeal, for an advisory, or abstract, opinion on their constitutionality. Many observers have faulted this system; on the ground that it is the basis for the politicization of the Canadian judiciary; or the judicialization of the Canadian politics. It may well be that the observers, who fault the Canadian reference procedure, are justified because, of late, most of the contentious issues, in Canadian politics, have reached the Supreme Court; through the said procedure.

A number of countries that permit a constitutional challenge, in anticipation that a bill, once enacted, may offend the constitution, often allow legislators, public officials, cabinet members, and Heads of State to initiate judicial review of proposed laws and hypothetical constitutional scenarios. This provides fertile ground for the judicialization of politics and the accompanying politicization of the judiciary. In France and Italy, for instance, the initiation of constitutional litigation, in constitutional courts, is limited to elected politicians. In other countries, such as Germany and Spain, elected officials may challenge proposed legislation through the abstract review.

Some countries reserve constitutional issues to constitutional courts only, while in others, such as Botswana, the lower courts, such as the High Court, can determine a constitutional dispute. A single judge of the High Court of Botswana is competent to deal with a constitutional matter. However, the law provides that an appeal, considering a constitutional matter, must be heard by a panel of five judges. The system that obtains in Botswana, and other countries that do not reserve constitutional questions to the Constitutional Courts and the Supreme Courts, whatever the case may be, makes the courts' impact on public policy more pronounced. To exemplify this, in 2017, a single judge of the High Court of Botswana practically closed down the highest court in the land, namely the Court of Appeal, on a number of grounds; including that some of the appointments of the justices of the Court of Appeal offended the country's constitution.

The debate that ensued, following that most controversial decision, demonstrated the impact of a decentralized constitutional review system on matters of public policy. It is quite plain that restricting the power to declare legislation and regulations unconstitutional to a constitutional court, or the apex court in the land, sharply reduces the number of occasions and range of policy issues on which courts can be invited to exercise judicial review.

It is also significant to note that even in countries that follow centralized constitutional review systems, administrative law remedies are often decentralized; thereby allowing the courts to render decisions that may be considered to trespass into the sphere of the executive. There are many cases in which, for instance, employment unions would challenge determinations of salary commissions, established by the executive, to determine salary grading in the public service. Where a court intervenes and sets aside such determinations, on the basis of irrationality, for example, the determination of the court is just as significant as that in countries which employ a decentralized review system.

In administrative justice, the law on standing, or the right to be heard by a court, is often used to control litigation that has an impact on public policy. Some countries have very rigid laws on standing; making it extremely difficult for public interest litigation to flourish, whilst other countries have very liberal laws on the same issue; making it easy to litigate on public interest matters. In some jurisdictions, the courts have insisted that where a matter may be decided on grounds other than constitutional ones, then that must be done. This is the case in Botswana. It would also seem that the U.S. Supreme Court will not hear a challenge to the constitutionality of legislation; unless all other possible legal paths and remedies have been exhausted.

Some legal commentators have attributed the incessant growth of judicial review, of executive and legislative decisions, to the rise of 'activist judges'; whose view of the law is coloured by their personal ideological inclinations. It is argued that activist judges appear too willing to supplement their perceived deficiencies of executive and legislative decisions; under the pretext of rendering decisions that are in accord with the dictates of justice. I refrain from offering an opinion on this; save to say that it is mainly those who take issue with the courts' seemingly elastic authority, in relation to the other arms of government, who may be the ardent proponents of the notion of 'activist judges'.

As indicated earlier, the starting point in considering what promotes, or does not promote the judicialization of politics, is the constitutional framework of a particular country. Kenya and South Africa have been given as examples of countries which have constitutions that expressly mandate judicial activism and, by extension, the judicialization of politics. Up to this point, there is quite a lot that has been said about the judicialization of politics. However, this discussion cannot be complete without the mention of the role of judges in the judicialization of politics. One thing that is definitely worth mentioning, in this regard, is that the attitude of judges plays a big part in the judicialization of politics. A restrained judiciary is always careful not to be seen to be 'meddlesome' in areas that are, usually, the province of other branches of government.

An increasing number of scholars suggest that judges do not behave, or even reach decisions, in a manner that is fundamentally different from those who are in other branches of government. These scholars posit that judges are just a different breed of politicians. They maintain that courts are political institutions not merely because they are politically constructed, but also because the determinants of judicial behaviour are not distinctly different from those of decision- making by other public officials. According to these scholars, judicial determinations, involving controversial political cases, are a function of many variables; such as knowledge, education, adherence to national meta-narratives, responsiveness to public opinion, personal ideological preferences, collegial considerations, prevalent attitudes within the legal profession, or strategic considerations; vis-à-vis other national decision-making bodies.

Anyone who is experienced, in the ways of the bench, would candidly accept that there are cases in which there is more than one possible answer to a legal question; and none of which answer is necessarily incorrect, or correct. A seasoned adjudicator will also accept that, out of the many possibly correct ones, the answer which must carry the day may lie in a strategic question; thus making the judge a strategic judicial operator. Viewed from this angle, it stands to reason that to dismiss the notion that judges, and courts, are strategic actors may not necessarily be correct. The reality is that judges are strategic actors; to the extent that they seek to maintain, or enhance, their institutional position, vis-à-vis other major national decision-making bodies, or to simply expand the ambit of their political influence and international profile. In the result, it may, at times, be narrow minded to analyze court decisions, especially those of the constitutional courts or other apex courts, as mere acts of professional apolitical jurisprudence; as doctrinal legalistic explanations of court rulings often suggests. This view is consistent with the comments by some legal scholars, in South Africa, following the 'Nkandla saga' in South Africa. This matter involved the construction of a private home, by the state, for the former South African President, Jacob Zuma; for millions of Rands.

After reading a number of the decisions of the Constitutional Court of South Africa, especially the one involving the Public Protector's Report on the 'Nkandla' saga, a legal scholar remarked that the Constitutional Court had correctly read the mood of the public, that considered the 'Nkandla' expenditure as a massive waste of tax payers' money; and that the court simply found the law which resonated with that mood. That line of reasoning may be, somewhat, cynical; but it illustrates the point that, sometimes, public opinion may play some role in judicial determinations; although not necessarily the text of the law. It is entirely conceivable, that courts may realize that there are circumstances in which they may be able to strengthen their own position; by extending the scope of their jurisprudence, and fortifying their status as crucial national policy-making bodies. These circumstances include the changing fates, or preferences, of other influential political actors, or the emergence of gaps in the institutional context within which they operate. This scenario usually results in national crises; and it is during such moments when the people, having lost confidence in the political leadership, look to the courts for deliverance. It goes without saying that while the courts are duty bound, at all times, to protect the rights of the people, this duty is heightened in a national crisis; and the courts must never fail the people who rely on them for deliverance.

Studies have shown that whilst it is not an everyday occurrence, the courts are often responsive to the political environment in which they operate. This may mean the courts deciding against the wishes of those who nominated them, such as in the case of the United States of America, or those who appointed them, as is the case in countries such as Botswana; where the Chief Justice is appointed by the President, directly, without the mechanism of the Judicial Service Commission. It may not be the easiest thing to do, since they are also but mere human beings, but judges have a duty to decide in accord with the merits, and justice, of any particular case that is brought before them; and not based on loyalty to the appointing, or nominating, authority.

While still on subject, it is of note that politicians often make the mistake of thinking that because they appointed judges, then those judges will be beholden to them; and do their every bidding. However, the truth of the matter is that once one is a judge, there are other factors, or considerations, that become far more important than past, or current, personal loyalties. An interesting trait about judges, and which I, daresay, my judicial colleagues may not be too thrilled that I have disclosed, is that judges generally seem to care more about their reputation, within their close social milieu, which includes court colleagues and the legal profession, than they do about what politicians and the appointing authorities do. It may be recalled that I mentioned, very early in this book, that judgeship is not for the faint hearted. What I have just alluded to, in terms of judges, sometimes, having to decide against their appointing, or nominating authorities, is one of the reasons why judges have to be bold in the execution of their functions. Quite obviously, a judge who decides contrary to the expectations of those who wield the political power may find himself, or herself, in an impossible, and even perilous, situation; even to the point of being hounded out of the judiciary in which they serve. But in all of this, judges must always remember that their loyalty lies with the constitution; which they swore to uphold at all times, and not depending on circumstances being favourable.

With the globalization of law, and the general inclination of most judges to do what is right and to ensure that justice is done, by learning from other jurisdictions, the matter of judicialization of politics may only grow. International and comparative law affords judges, and the courts, the opportunity to increase their symbolic power and international prestige; by fostering its alignment with a growing community of liberal democratic nations who are engaged in judicial review and rights-based discourses.

At the end of the day, there are a number of factors that explain the growing phenomenon of judicialization of politics. Judicialization of politics is a function of many factors; such as the political culture, the nature and character of the legal system and the attitude of judges, themselves, to their core mandate. The political culture is relevant because in countries where democracy is deficient, and institutions to support democracy are weak, or non-existent, and there is a price to pay for bold innovative judicial decisions, judges may feel constrained to go as far as they may wish; for fear of political backlash. One may ask, in view of this, that what became of the assertion that judgeship is not for the faint hearted. The simple answer is that my views on this score remain unchanged. However, and as I mentioned before, judges are only human; and not all of them may wish to face political backlash in the name of not being faint of heart. This is especially true in jurisdictions where the political environment may hostile.

We should not run away from the fact that the courts are, first and foremost, political institutions and that, like any other such institutions, they do not operate in an institutional, or ideological, vacuum. It would be incorrect to attempt to understand how the courts operate outside the concrete social, political, and economic struggles that shape a given political system. The growing power of the courts, which have been conferred on them as the guardians of the constitution, must be located in the context of a fast evolving society; that aspires to higher ideals of democracy. In many respects, the judicialization of politics must be regarded as simply part of the growth stages of democracy. By its very nature, democracy entails the establishment of some form of separation of powers among the major branches of government. It also entails the presence of a set of procedural governing rules, and decision-making processes, to which all political actors are required to adhere.

In countries that subscribe to constitutional democracies, as is the trend nowadays, it is inevitable that the boundaries between the three branches of government should continue to be blurred; and the relationship strained. When courts are called upon to review and determine whether particular acts, or omissions, of the executive offend the constitution, and they do so, it does not mean that they are meddling in politics. To the contrary, the courts are simply doing their job. Where any challenge is brought, that would offend against the separation of powers, the courts would say so; and if a challenge doesn't offend against separation of powers, then courts will listen to the parties; and pronounce themselves accordingly.

Another development that explains the judicialization of politics, which is also both a pre-requisite and by-product of a democratic society, is the emergence of an enlightened civil society that takes the issue of human rights seriously; and is also willing to demonstrate, and picket, for the purposes of calling attention to the violation of human rights, by governments. Nowadays civil society has become very litigious. For example, in South Africa, civil society has won decisive, and important, victories against a government that was unwilling to roll out HIV/AIDS medication.

In Kenya, the rights of Tuberculosis (TB) patients which were, for a long time, denied by the executive, have been recognized and enforced by the courts. Civil society often litigates to advance, and expand, the rights of people and, in the course of doing so, both informs and educates. This may yield what may be termed 'judicialization from below'.

Civil Society Organizations (CSOs), including political movements, have historically turned to litigation to advance the causes that they believe in. The resulting litigation is best described as strategic. In this context, litigation is strategic in the sense that it attempts to persuade the courts to use their learning, and integrity, to expand the democratic space; or to enforce the rights, especially, of the marginalized and vulnerable groups. Strategic litigation, in my respectful view, casts CSOs as some kind of a radical, social critic of the unsatisfactory status quo, and also as groups which litigate in order to exhort the courts to replace the present, unjust, reality with a just, and equal, future. Strategic litigation emphasizes the vision of justice as a continual struggle; rather than as a set of legal norms or procedures. Such litigation does not, necessarily, mourn over lost cases; mainly because its primary purpose is to advance a vision of a better society.

Civil Society Organizations which use the courts to advance the vision of an equal society must regard law as a process of struggle, where they would be defeats and victories along the way; and even causalities. Litigation, in terms of this view, arises from a conflict between a status quo that is unjust, and civil society's vision to create a better society; in which rights of all persons are respected. In my mind, for any Civil Society Organization that is engaged in the task of attaining a better society, the symbol of justice should not just be the traditional scales, connoting a calm and detached balancing of the scales; it should, instead, be an imagery of a turbulent cascading river.

Strategic litigation uses the courts as a forum of rational engagement, especially with respect to the enforcement of certain rights; that may be politically unpopular. In addition to winning legal battles, which may have immediate and concrete benefits, strategic litigation also serves a very important educational purpose. For all their usefulness in advancing the vision of an equal society, Civil Society Organizations must, however, understand the limitations of the law; and must know that it cannot be a panacea for all societal ills. They must, equally, realize that much as it can be a force for good, the law can, in equal measure, be a force for bad. This notwithstanding, Civil Society Organizations should take comfort in the fact that the law, and the courts, can be engaged, successfully, to move the agenda of a better society forward.

Civil society must appreciate that even losing litigation can be an important mechanism for a narrative that is central to the creation of a better society. When judgments are passed, which dismiss cases in which Civil Society sought to bring about a fairer and better society, not all is lost; as what is left behind is a narrative of resistance. The lessons learned, by future generations, is not that the case was lost, but that a civil society grouping, and their lawyers, found the courage, energy and creativity to resist injustice; in the face of overwhelming odds.

It is a well-recognized fact that the extent to which people enjoy rights is often limited by individuals' inability to invoke those rights through strategic litigation. It follows, therefore, that constitutional recognition counts for nothing if the democratic space to organize is closed, and freedom of expression is muzzled. To this extent, only a vibrant and well organized Civil Society, that is capable of bringing the masses to collectively demand what is right, can better guarantee democratic outcomes. These may take the form of

a. galaxy of rights-advocacy organizations ranging from religious groups, students and workers movements; to name only but a few. Even when they are operating from within a constitution that comprehensively entrenches rights, judges,

b. alone, cannot guarantee democracy and human rights. The effectiveness of human rights provisions, in planting the seeds of social change in a given polity, is largely contingent upon the existence of a support structure for legal mobilization and, more generally, socio-cultural conditions that are hospitable for judicialization from below.

c. It must also be noted that Civil Society will not engineer the judicialization of politics from below, if they are convinced that the courts are not independent. However, it is also possible that even where they perceive the courts to be captured, by the executive or other forces, Civil Society may still litigate, if nothing else but to send the message to the larger populace; that their judicial institutions are not fit for their purpose. There is always a danger that where Civil Society and the greater majority of a people, in a community, reach the conclusion that the courts, and the law, can no longer serve their interests, they may take the law into their own hands. That is why it is important that the institutions meant to support democracy must always endeavour, even under difficult circumstances, to discharge their constitutional mandate.

d. In some countries, the courts may find themselves walking a tight rope; in so far as judicialization from the bottom may be concerned. This is so in instances where it is the main opposition political parties which frequent the courts in order to challenge governmental decisions. In South Africa, it is fair to say that the main opposition, the Democratic Alliance, has had a fair share of victories against the government; on a number of high profile and politically charged controversies. To their credit, the South African courts have, steadfastly, applied the law; and refused to be swayed by the identity of the litigant. Many African

e. jurisdictions would do well to take a leaf from the resolve of the South African courts in upholding the constitution; for the good of the society which they serve.

f. In many respects, judicialization of politics is largely a function of concrete choices, interests, or strategic considerations by those involved in strategic litigation. The opposition may seek to judicialize politics for a number of reasons; including to simply harass and obstruct governments in their development agendas. There are also instances in which the opposition may resort to litigation in an attempt to enhance their media exposure; regardless of the actual outcome of litigation. Where any strategic litigation brought forth by members of Civil Society or the opposition succeeds, it amounts to a very important validation of their complaint, because the court would have taken time to assess the dispute; and come to a favourable conclusion. In most constitutional democracies, the courts enjoy greater public legitimacy and support than, virtually, all other political institutions.

g. Inspite of all the positive things that judicialization of politics may bring, it comes with its own costs. Where courts are perceived to overreach, or as being overly political, the judicialization of politics may, in the long run, undermine their legitimacy. This is particularly possible when political parties start mobilizing, and agitating, their members to regard the courts as political enemies; whose main aim is to engineer regime change, by their judgments. In the early part of 2017, some members of the African National Congress, in Durban, went on a march; demanding that the courts should not meddle in the president's power to re-shuffle his cabinet.

h. Quite often, a government that perceives itself to be under attack from the judiciary may take a number of self-preservation measures; such as the harassment of judges, sponsoring unjustified impeachments, intimidating judges, clipping jurisdictional boundaries and judicial review powers, appointing compliant judges, blocking those judicial candidates deemed to be undesirable, reversing courts' rulings and using their majority, in the legislatures, to launch attacks on the independence of the judiciary and the rule of law. This is more pronounced in countries with democratic deficiencies, or those countries which are ruled by dictatorships.

i. Whatever may be said on the subject, it cannot be denied that law and politics have a close relationship. Some scholars contend that law is politics by another name. This school of thought also contends that judges are just politicians, in flowing robes, who fake neutrality. However, according classical democratic theory, the law is supposed to be separate from politics and, where necessary, it can, and should, correct the failings of politics. Furthermore, the law is also viewed as technical and neutral, applied by the judges who are professionals in their trade and are, most certainly, neither partisan nor part of the factions that are running the state. In terms of this theory, when a dispute serves before the courts, the duty of the judges is to preside over the dispute in an independent, and impartial, manner; while applying pre-existing rules.

j. In a functional democracy, it is accepted that decisions of the courts, being independent and impartial, must be respected by all. Citizens and the political leaders accept that they have no legitimate claim to influence the courts to decide in a particular way and that the courts, unlike the

k. legislature, cannot be lobbied to decide in a particular way. If there is any lobbying, at all, it may be a protest that articulates the views of the protestors but, then, the judges are trained to ignore such influences; as irrelevant to the task at hand.

l. In the logic of democratic theory, members of the legislature who are not performing may be recalled, or be voted out of office at the next elections. This is not so with the judges; whose tenure must be secure; as part of the necessary condition for them to be able to decide controversial issues, before them, independently and without any fear of removal. In the contemporary society, in which we live, it is considered simplistic to suggest that politics must be confined only to the legislature and the executive; but not the judiciary. No one doubts that some court decisions may seem like political decisions, and are possibly influenced by the political inclinations of the individual judge.

m. In conclusion, I wish to reiterate that the phenomena of judicialization of politics and politicization of the judiciary are a reality of our time. As the courts continue to assert their authority, as the ultimate guardians of the constitution, there is bound to be tension. Such tension is not, necessarily, a bad thing. It may, actually, be useful as a check, for the purposes of each arm of government keeping to within its lane; in terms of its constitutional functions and obligations. In many ways, the tension that arises from the courts asserting their authority as custodians of the constitution is axiomatic to the constitutional order that espouses democracy, human rights and the rule of law. In the last two decades, the judicialization of politics has extended to well beyond the now 'standard' judicialization of policy-making,

n. to encompass questions of pure politics such as electoral processes and outcomes, regime legitimacy and executive prerogatives. These developments reflect the demise of the 'political question' doctrine, and mark a transition to what has been termed 'juristocracy'.

o. The era of juristocracy carries with it certain obligations by the judiciary. It calls for the avoidance of judicial adventurism. It also calls for judges to be knowledgeable, and skilled, and for them to know when to intervene or not intervene, in the actions of the other wings of government; bearing in mind that the last thing that any judiciary would want to do, is to undermine its legitimacy, by eroding public confidence in the courts; as independent and impartial arbiters of the nation.

CONCLUSION

In conclusion, it is fair to conclude that justice, as the ultimate objective of law, is extremely important for the orderly development of society. Public confidence in the ability of the courts to administer justice competently, fairly and without fear, or favour, is the life blood of any functional system of the administration of justice. As the guardians of the constitution, judges are the trustees of the rule of law. This means that they have a duty to ensure, at all times, that no individual, whether a street sweeper or a president is above the law; and that both are treated equally in the eyes of the law. Judges must carry out this duty on behalf of the public; who delegated judicial power to them.

It is often said public confidence is the life blood of an independent judiciary because that is the only basis for its moral authority. The judiciary has no purse to finance its operations, nor does it have police officers and soldiers to enforce its will. The executive arm of the state must enforce its orders, because it knows that the price for not doing so, which may come from the public, may be too costly. Alexander Hamilton, one of the founders of the American Republic, has recognized that in a body politic whose legislative, executive and judicial powers are separated, the legislature controls the purse, the executive controls force and the judiciary neither.

Without public confidence in the ability of the courts to be true guardians of the constitution, the rule of law would not endure. It would ultimately collapse and chaos would reign supreme. Without the rule of law, nothing would be predictable. Business would flee and so would jobs. Victims of crime, in a society without the rule of law, would be vulnerable and would be left with no choice but to take the law into their own hands. In the absence of the rule of law, there would be no peace and order; which every society needs in order to develop.

The opposite to its absence is that where there is the rule of law, business is likely to take root and create sustainable jobs, fundamental rights and freedoms would be respected and an orderly, and peaceful, society would develop; thereby guaranteeing maximum happiness for the greatest number of people.

Judiciaries only enjoy the confidence of the people, if the people believe that the judges are honest, competent, incorruptible, independent and impartial. It helps if these principles are firmly secured in the constitution. A cardinal point to remember, in any discussion on the judiciary, is that impartiality is a supreme judicial virtue. This is clearly illustrated in the concept of judicial impartiality, which is embodied by an icon; i.e. the blind folded goddess of justice holding the sword and scales of justice. The sword represents the rigour of justice, which does not hesitate to punish. The blindfold represents the idea that political views, sympathy and other irrational considerations are very bad guides to dispensing justice. A blindfolded justice cannot see who comes before her, and hence, cannot be impressed by the power of the litigants, or witnesses, who may seek to intimidate her.

The concept of judicial impartiality, as captured by the goddess of justice, is the fountain of public confidence. But engendering public confidence does not, automatically, come from the dress code of a judge, namely a wig and a gown. It comes from the way judges conduct themselves. According to Justice Barak, of the Supreme Court of Israel, public confidence in the judiciary can be maintained in the following ways:

> The judge ought to be aware of his or her power, and its limits, because given the immense power that judges have, there is always the potential to abuse it; A judge must admit his, or her mistakes, because they are human; and do commit mistakes. Judges must have the humility, and courage, to accept those mistakes and correct them;
>
> Judges must display modesty and absence of arrogance;
>
> Judges must be honest.

To the above list, one may add kindness, patience, integrity and the pursuit of excellence in one's work; that is to say, the unceasing drive to deliver judgments that are well reasoned, in time. Judges must, at all times, conduct themselves in a manner befitting the exalted office that they hold. I believe that judgeship is some kind of priesthood. The way judges carry themselves, both in public and private spheres, must engender confidence and trust. Judgeship, as it is often said, is not a job; but a way of life. The pursuit of material things in the form of fame and publicity are alien to judgeship. The defining characteristic of judgeship is selfless service to the community to achieve justice through law and also to breathe life into the constitution; and ensure that the constitution represents both the current generation and those generations yet to be born.

A judge's decisions must, at all times, be able to withstand rigorous scrutiny. A judgement must typically reflect the neutrality, impartiality and independence that define the judiciary, itself. As one of the three co-equal arms of government the judiciary must enjoy the same status as other arms of the state.

As this book has shown, the role of the judiciary is an expansive one. The power of the judiciary, to review the exercise of public authority, is growing rapidly. The courts have the power to overrule the decisions of the other elected arms of the state; if their decisions contravene the constitution. History has shown that if this power of review is not exercised with care, it can create unnecessary tension and undermine the integrity of the state.

In order to encourage a harmonious relationship between the three co-equal arms of the state, most constitutions either expressly, or by necessary implication, contemplate interaction amongst the three branches of government. This interaction, often called the constitutional dialogue, is rooted in the obligation to respect the constitution. Part of the obligation to respect the constitution may drive judges in the direction of making laws, a topic that was discussed in the earlier chapters of this book. It has also been shown that there was a time when it was considered some kind of judicial heresy to suggest that judges make law. However, a total shift in this paradigm is that it is now readily conceded that they do. Lord Denning was famous for having been a legal reformer; who often made law in his decisions. He referred to those judges who were more restrained as 'timorous souls'. Some accused him of making the law uncertain, and it is reported that he was once asked, by a student, to make no more changes to the law until the exams were over. While there is unlikely ever to be another Lord Denning, one thing that remains unchanged is that judges, throughout the ages, will always be expected to carry out their juridical functions to expectation; and maintain public confidence in the judiciary.

SELECTED REFERENCES BIBLIOGRAPHY

Cases

Attorney General v Dow 1992 BLR 119

Attorney General v Thuto Rammoge & 19 Others 2016 CACGB - 128–14

Brown v The Board of Education of Topeka, 347, US 483 (1954)

BTR Industries South Africa (Pty) Ltd and Others v Metal and Allied Workers' Union and Another (151/89) [1992] ZASCA 85; 1992 (3) *SA* 673 (AD); [1992] 4

Candler v Crane, Christmas & Co (1951) 2 KB 164.

Dykes v Hosemann 743 F.2d 1488.

Floyd v Barker 77 ENG. Rep (1607) http://www.saflii.org/za/cases/ZASCA/1992/85.html

Gitari v Non-Governmental Organizations Board Petition NO 440 of 2013 (Kenya).

Judicial Services Commission v Mbalu Mutava Civil Appeal no. 52 of 2014 (2015) eKLR http://kenyalaw.org/caselaw/cases/view/109097/

Kanane v The State 2003 (2) BLR 67 (CA)

Mafeela v the State 1996 BLR 15 (CA) http://www.elaws.
gov.bw/desplaylrpage.php?id=1453&dsp=2

Magaya v Magaya 1999 (3) LRC 35.

Minister of Interior & Another v Harris & Others 1952 (2)
SA 428 (AD).

Mmusi & Others v Ramantele & Anothers 2012 (2) BLR
590.

Obergefell v Hodges 576 US (2015).

President of RSA v RSA Rugby Football Union CCT 16/98
[1999] ZACC 11;2000 (1) SA 1 10 1999 (10) BLLR
1059 10 September 1999.

http://www.saflii.org/za/cases/ZACC/1999/11.html
Penrice v Dickinson 945 AD 16

Raila Odinga & Another v Independent Electoral and
Boundaries Commission & 2 Others 2017 eKLR
(Presidential Petition No. 1 of 2017).

Regional Magistrate Du Preez v Walker 1976 4 SA 849 (A)
Rossouw v Sachs 1964 (2) SA 551.

R v Mcllkenny, Hunter, Walker, Callaghan, Hill & Power
(1991)93 Crim. App. R. 287.

R v Oak 1986 1 SCR 103.

R v Valente [1985] 2.S.C.R 673. Sirros v Moore 375 US
335 (1964)

Stump v Sparkman 435 US 349 (1978).

Tiger Eye PI (JI/9/2016)[2016]GHASC 80 (27 October 2016) https://ghalii.org/gh/judgment/supreme-court/2016/80

S v Roberts and Others (CC 20/2011) [2012] ZAECPEHC 72; 2013

SACR 369 (ECP) (27 September 2012) http://www.saflii. org/za/cases/ZAECPEHC/2012/72.html

South African Constitution Act No.108 of 2006.

Valente v Queen [1985] 2 S.C.R 673 http://www.judicial-ethics.umontreal.ca/en/jurisprudence/documents/ VALENTE_AN GLAIS.pdf

Books

Benjamin Cardazo, The Nature of the Judicial Process (1921) Yale University Press

Elexander Hamilton, John Lay, The Federalist Papers (1788).

Han Kelsen Pure Theory of Law (1967) University of California Press.

HLA Hart: The Concept of Law (1961) Clavedon Law Services.

John Austin: Province of Jurisprudence Determined 1861, London:

John Murray Albemarle Street.

John Rawls: A Theory of Justice (1971) Havard University Press.

Oagile Key Dingake, Constitutionalism and the Rule of Law in Botswana (2011) Mmegi Publishing House.

Oliver Wendell Holmes Jr, The Common Law (1991) (Revised Edition) Dover Publications.

Ronald Dwarkin: Taking Rights Seriously (1977) Havard University Press.

William Blackstone: The Commentaries on the Laws of England

1765 – 1769 (Claredon Press: Oxford).

International Legal Instruments

African Charter on Human and Peoples Rights (Banjul Charter) 1981.

Convention on the Elimination of All Forms of Discrimination Against Women (CEDAW) (1981).

Universal Declaration of Human Rights of 1948.

2002 Bangalore Principles of Judicial Conduct https://www.unodc.org/pdf/crime/corruption/judicial_group/Ba ngalore_principles.pdf

The Principles and Guidelines on the Right to a Fair Trial and Legal Assistance in Africa

http://www.achpr.org/files/instruments/principles-guidelines-right-fair-trial/achpr33_guide_fair_trial_legal_assistance_2003_eng.pdf

The United Nations Basic Principles on the Independence of the Judiciary, Lawyers and Judges

https://ijrcenter.org/un-special-procedures/special-rapporteur-on-the-independence-of-judges-and-lawyers/

Internet sources

Commonwealth Latimer Principles

http://thecommonwealth.org/history-of-the-commonwealth/latimer-principles

http://legalbrief.co.za/media/filestore/2017/06/Law_Society_of_ Botswana_v_President_High_Court.pdf

Laurance M. Hyde, Jr

https://scholarship.law.nd.edu/ndlr/vol30/iss2/3/

Masuku case

http://www.southernafricalitigationcentre.org/2011/09/29/swa ziland-justice-thomas-masuku-fired/

Michael Dingake

www.sahistory.org.za>Biographies   www.sahistory.or.za/people/michael-kitso-dingake

Dingake appointed a Judge in New Papua Guinea www.mmegi.bw/index.php?aid=74128&dir+2018/january126

The International Bar Association Minimum Standards of Judicial Independence

https://www.icj.org/wpcontent/uploads/2014/10/IBA_
    Resolutio   ns_Minimum_Standards_of_Judicial_
    Independence_1982.pdf

The United Nations Special Rapporteur on Independence
    of Judges

https://ijrcenter.org/un-special-procedures/special-
    rapporteur-on-the-independence-of-judges-and-
    lawyers/